DIGITAL DARWINISM

ALSO BY EVAN I. SCHWARTZ
WEBONOMICS

EVAN I. SCHWARTZ

BROADWAY BOOKS
NEW YORK

DIGITAL DARWINISM

BREAKTHROUGH BUSINESS
STRATEGIES FOR SURVIVING IN THE
CUTTHROAT WEB ECONOMY

Broadway Books titles may be purchased for business or promotional use or for special sales. For information, please write to: Special Markets Department, Random House, Inc., 1540 Broadway, New York, NY 10036.

BROADWAY BOOKS and its logo, a letter B bisected on the diagonal, are trademarks of Broadway Books, a division of Random House, Inc.

Visit our website at www.broadwaybooks.com

Library of Congress Cataloging-in-Publication Data
Schwartz, Evan I.
Digital Darwinism : seven breakthrough business strategies for surviving in the cutthroat Web economy / by Evan I. Schwartz. — 1st ed.
p.   cm.
A sequel to his Webonomics.
"Directory of websites": p. 199.
Includes index.
ISBN 0-7679-0333-1 (hc)
1.   Internet marketing.   2.   Electronic commerce.   3. World Wide Web (Information retrieval system)   I. Schwartz, Evan I. Webonomics.   II.   Title.   III.   Title: Strategies for surviving in the cutthroat Web economy.
HF5415.1265.S383   1999
658'.054678—dc21   98-52199
                                                           CIP

FIRST EDITION

99 00 01 02 03 10 9 8 7 6 5 4 3 2 1

DESIGNED BY JENNIFER ANN DADDIO

TO MY PARENTS
AND TO THEIR GRANDDAUGHTER, LILY

CONTENTS

DIGITAL DARWINISM

INTRODUCTION:
FRENETIC EVOLUTION

We will now discuss, in little more detail, the struggle for existence.
—CHARLES DARWIN, *The Origin of Species*

When Charles Darwin presented his theory of evolution in 1859, he described a world in which only the fittest survive, a world in which species must constantly adapt to their changing environment or face extinction, a world in which organisms must continue to grow in a profitable direction and develop new skills and traits or perish, a world in which life-forms must look around and learn with whom to cooperate and with whom to compete, a world in which the surrounding conditions for life can, suddenly and drastically, improve or take a turn for the worse. Darwin even wrote that we are all "bound together in a complex web of relations."

This lexicon applies unmistakably to the digital business landscape now flourishing and mutating across the World Wide Web. "Many more individuals of each species are born than can possibly survive," Darwin wrote. "Consequently, there is a frequently recurring struggle for existence, and it follows that any being, if it varies however slightly in any manner profitable to itself under the complex conditions of life, will have a better chance of surviving, and thus be naturally selected." And just as Darwin observed that competition for food and resources leads to principles of natural evo-lution, we can see that brutal market forces in the increasingly cut-throat Web economy lead to new strategies for economic survival.

Indeed, the Web is in the throes of an especially frenetic evo-lution. As an environment that can sustain economic life, the Web has given birth to entirely new species of start-ups and enterprises that could not have existed previously. These new economic organ-isms are, in turn, forcing older corporate species to evolve in new ways, producing new business models and characteristics necessary for their own survival.

Still, evolution takes time to manifest itself in a significant way. In the natural world, often it takes thousands of years for ma-jor or even slight changes to become apparent. The Web may be a universe of digital information in which companies can change their appearance and switch their survival plans in a matter of weeks, but evolution writ large still requires a more significant time frame to produce outcomes, results, effects, and lessons learned the hard way.

We are already moving beyond the commercial Web's era as a marshland for single-cell organisms. Corporate creatures founded on one simple, untested idea—selling a certain product or service online, for instance—have been happily splashing about in the early Web's primordial soup, perhaps not realizing that they are re-ally just simmering themselves before drowning or becoming somebody else's lunch. At the same time, their rivals are clawing their way to prosperity, developing higher forms of intelligence, and inventing breakthrough business tactics especially suited to their swiftly shifting surroundings.

What will the Web economy look like as evolution escalates and we witness real conflicts, surprises, new developmental stages, and turning points?

Will it be uncertain? Absolutely.

Unpredictable? Most assuredly.

Unusual? Rather so.

Unruly? Quite often.

Unsustainable? It has been thus far.

Uncluttered? Far from it.

Undramatic? No chance.

Unsafe? Bloody awful.

Unrewarding? Not if you listen closely.

In the Beginning

In various forms, the Internet has existed since the late 1960s. But the emergence of the World Wide Web transformed the Internet's stark environment of drab databases into a fertile, living-color infosphere inhabited by vast numbers of consumers and companies. While the Web was conceived in 1989 as a scientific data-sharing tool, the commercial browser software that appeared beginning in 1993 provided the first inkling that far more could be accomplished here. And as a serious field of endeavor, Web commerce came into being in 1995, the year Netscape's stock went public in a *bit bang*, if you will, that ignited interest and sparked new forms of economic life around the world.

Since then, the Web has evolved with mind-numbing quickness, achieving mass acceptance faster than any other technology in modern history. It has made its way into the homes of one-third of the U.S. population and ended up in the hands of 100 million users worldwide in a shorter span of time than even personal computers managed to accomplish the same feat. It has infiltrated people's daily lives faster than the telephone or the fax machine, faster than radio or television, faster than the automobile, even faster than electricity itself.

At first the Web was an unformed mass of frivolous expression, free publications, corporate brochures, and piles of pornography.

People treated it as if they were early cave dwellers witnessing fire for the first time. They were simply afraid of it—afraid to send their credit card numbers over it, afraid to trust any information on it, afraid that their privacy would be obliterated, afraid to let their kids near it. As a result, virtually all of the original predictions and forecasts for actually doing business on this untested terrain were, in retrospect, quite humble.

But looking back, its evolution seemed to progress in a logical order. Fear naturally gave way to experimentation. High-tech early adopters began downloading software and researching new computer and networking gear. They began placing real orders for PCs and Internet traffic-routing hardware that soon added up to millions of dollars per day in revenue for some companies. Physical software stores closed up shop and reopened their doors on the Web, while other computer makers scrambled to alter their business models to sell online. In the $500-billion computer and software industry, buying through traditional channels may soon become the exception.

Successful experimentation soon led to confidence. Frequent travelers attempted to book their airline flights on the Web's numerous new online reservation systems. They entered their credit card numbers and reliably received their tickets. The airlines then began encouraging online booking as a cost-saving move, providing frequent flier points as special incentives. Within several short years, about 5 percent of the massive $126 billion in domestically booked travel reservations were being sold online. And that percentage is expected to be as high as 25 percent just a few years into the new millennium.

Confidence inspired trust. What first captured the public's imagination was online sales of books and CDs. Literature and music are in many ways the repositories of culture itself, so when people began shopping for these items on the Web, the digital commerce landscape began to radiate a shiny new aura. With online sales of books and music already surpassing $1 billion annually, those industries have begun to restructure themselves for the day when an even more significant share of their business would be transacted this way.

Trust led to faith. The public began taking seriously the product and pricing information presented on the Web. And so it became a primary research forum for big-ticket purchases—from cars, to homes, to corporate procurement—transactions that often ended up being completed offline. A new breed of online auto-buying services already drives more than $12 billion in new car sales, and they're causing the $1-trillion global auto industry to begin changing the way its products are marketed and delivered to consumers.

Faith led to mass acceptance. When you consider that the Web has already become a popular new tool for finding a job, for performing banking and personal finance tasks, for getting global and local news and information, and for dozens of other everyday chores, you can begin to see how shortsighted the early skeptics were. At the dawn of the Web economy, few would have predicted that members of 20 percent of all U.S. households would be shopping the Net by the end of the century and that a $250-billion online consumer marketplace could loom on the immediate horizon.

The emergence of new entrepreneurial life-forms has attracted the attention of the corporate giants. The world's biggest companies are now gazing toward a future in which much if not most of their purchasing, invoicing, document exchange, and logistics will be transferred from stand-alone computer networks connected by people, paper, and phone calls to a seamless Web that spans the globe and connects more than a billion computing devices. Industries as diverse as commercial real estate, electronics, office supplies, and food services have begun to settle the new terrain by constructing sophisticated business-to-business applications.

As a result, online business-to-business spending is expected to explode, becoming the centerpiece of a mind-boggling multitrillion-dollar Web economy. As even technologically lagging industries such as healthcare, education, and legal services begin to do more and more business over the Web, the opportunities have become too big for anyone to ignore. Add it all up and electronic commerce has already surpassed 2 percent of the gross domestic product in the United States. Within a few years that figure is expected to soar past 10 percent and account for 20 percent or more of the total economic activity in many of the world's top industrial nations.

But even as life on the Web flourishes on the surface, danger lurks beneath. With the raw fear largely gone, with the primitive experimentation mostly left behind, with the original novelty of Internet shopping and e-commerce wearing off, with the technology no longer appearing so futuristic, the digital business environment has taken on an air of indispensability, of inevitability.

Here is where the most intense struggle for existence begins. When just about *everybody* is convinced that just about *anybody* can sell just about *anything* via the Web, when success in the Web economy becomes a foregone conclusion, when confidence leads to overconfidence and then to sheer euphoria, we naturally progress to the next stage of emotion: one of pure greed and naked ambition.

Such passions are hardly foreign to Darwinian evolution or the world of business—in fact, they make the marketplace function quite well. But as Darwin himself forewarned, don't be surprised when some of today's most dominant creatures are rendered helpless in the face of rapid, unforeseen change. "So profound is our ignorance, and so high our presumption," the British naturalist wrote, "that we marvel when we hear of the extinction of an organic being. . . . [But] every being must suffer destruction during some period of its life."

Following the Money

Just as we cannot understand natural evolution without studying how plants and animals obtain their food, we cannot comprehend the complex evolution of the Web economy without following its main form of sustenance: money.

Since 1996 venture capitalists have seeded thousands of information technology start-ups with more than $4 billion each year, by far the biggest years in venture capital history. An even larger number of major companies have invested even more prodigious amounts of money in their own internal Web commerce ventures. "Anyone with an Internet idea could get funding," says a partner with Kleiner Perkins Caufield & Buyers, Silicon Valley's most elite venture firm. "We've been in an anomalous period," another Internet venture capitalist tells me. "The amount of money to invest exceeds the number of solid, investment-worthy businesses."

In any case, these financial resources are not provided on a philanthropic basis. Like successful parents siring offspring, venture capitalists propagate certain traits and characteristics in their young. In return for the cash, the venture firm takes an equity interest in the start-up, typically a 10- to 40-percent ownership position. The venture firm is constantly seeking an exit strategy, an opportunity to get its money back times ten or—in rare cases—a hundred times or more. This occurs when the company is sold to another or sells shares of itself to the public. "If I were teaching a class in venture capital, I'd say the payback period should be three to five years," says yet another venture capitalist. "But in this environment, it has been shortened to two years or less."

Yet it is the *way* in which some Web start-ups have made both their executives and their venture backers so fabulously wealthy that leaves us convinced that we are just beginning to scale the evolutionary ladder. One venture-backed start-up, an online video store called Reel.com, decided that it would sell copies of the megahit *Titanic* for $9.99 per copy immediately upon its release, despite the fact that it cost about $15 per copy to buy the cassettes wholesale from Paramount, the studio that made the film. Reel.com proceeded to spend millions of dollars advertising the promotion in the mass media and the Web.

Not surprisingly, hundreds of thousands of *Titanic* fans flocked to the site to purchase the video. And Reel.com started burning through $600,000 per week until it had lost nearly all of the $7.5 million in venture capital funds that it had raised. But before the company had a chance to drop dead, a giant video rental chain called Hollywood Entertainment decided to acquire it for $100 million, creating a new hybrid company in the process. "All I know is that I made a lot of money from that deal," says Michael Barach, a former partner with Reel.com's primary venture investor.

This business model—or lack thereof—has been in evidence across a wide swath of the Web. The underlying idea—that as long as a company is on the Web and perhaps attracting lots of traffic, it will eventually, ultimately, somehow, turn into a real business—has been replicated across many Web species. Consider these telling examples of investors' blind faith in the power of the Net:

- The stock market capitalization of America Online has at least temporarily exceeded that of Walt Disney, while eBay's eclipsed RJR Nabisco's, Yahoo's became bigger than Boeing's, and Amazon.com's grew greater than that of retailers Borders, Barnes & Noble, Kmart, and J.C. Penney combined.

- K-Tel, an outfit known for selling cheesy records on late-night infomercials in the 1970s, simply issued a press release saying it will begin selling CDs online, and its stock leapt tenfold within days.

- A gnat of a company losing $9 million per year publishing technical trade magazines online adopted the mystical name

EarthWeb and staged one of the top three initial public offering (IPO) debuts in history.

▶ A cash-hemorrhaging entity called TheGlobe.com that offers free home pages and chat services has no business model to speak of, yet its stock multiplied 606 percent, an all-time IPO record, on its very first day of trading.

Readers might wonder: Why not just cut to the chase? Open a site called dollarbills.com. Offer to ship crisp, newly minted, legally tender $1 notes to buyers for 85 cents each, including shipping and handling. Such a company would no doubt attract millions of new customers from all over the world overnight. It would build a valuable brand name. It could even sell millions of dollars' worth of advertising. Patent the concept. Pitch it to venture capitalists. Alert the media. Call the investment bankers. Then take it public.

In a tangible sense, the Web has been perpetuating its own excess. In the flick of a ticker, low-cost online stock trading has grown into a prime pastime. Like airline reservation systems, securities trading had long been an electronic process; the Web simply extended it all the way to the end customer. Within the span of three years, online trading went from accounting for 0 percent to 25 percent of all retail stock trading. Day traders, panic buyers, and greater fools are now able to buy and unload shares more quickly and cheaply than ever before. Online traders, on average, execute four times the number of transactions as traditional investors, and volatile Internet stocks have been their highest-volume bets.

As an investment phenomenon, the Web is certainly not without precedent. In the late 1980s cable television was all set to revolutionize shopping as we know it, and stock in the Home Shopping Network "had gone from 18 to 133 in the time it takes to say 'cubic zirconium,'" notes James J. Cramer, president of TheStreet.com, an online investment guide. "Then it suffered the most brutal, protracted decline to single digits that I have ever witnessed." It has since been swallowed up by USA Networks.

But the underlying value of the Web as a marketplace for serious business makes it unfair to compare this early wave of speculation to that earlier episode or even to the infamous Dutch tulip bulb craze of the early 1600s. The Web is much more than a mass delusion. Smaller but similar speculative bubbles expanded and popped during the early days of the telegraph in the 1880s, radio in the 1920s, and the biotech business circa 1990. Yes, most high-risk investments collapse, but some of them turn into super-winners, and the industries they represent usually turn out to be very real indeed. Even shopping over cable—although no longer considered revolutionary—has grown into a multibillion-dollar business.

So when something new happens, when something breathtakingly big happens, when an entire digital industrial complex screeches into being out of nowhere and starts moving and shaking as if it's going to take over the entire economic stratosphere, the response that follows is a natural one: Hypesters start to hype, corporations start to splurge and merge, and investors start to get hungry. They want to own some of it, sure. But not only that. More than that. They can't *not* own some. They don't want to look foolish—so foolish that they were actually the only living and breathing weekly newsmagazine readers in the late 1990s who hadn't snagged some Yahoo! or Amazon.com while the gettin' was good.

Environmental Change

Natural checks in the system will always guarantee that such booms can't last. Some of the hottest Internet start-ups, if they continue to grow their market valuations at anywhere near past rates, will before long be the most highly valued companies in the world. By ignoring normal investment metrics, such as price-to-earnings ratios, investors have allowed these companies to proliferate like species of jungle animals without any natural predators. "Lighten any check, and the number will almost instantaneously increase to any amount," Darwin noted.

Systematic checks in this system could include a sudden drop or rebalancing of the food supply (in terms of fewer investment dollars or a far greater number of investment-worthy Web stocks), the sudden appearance of new predators (in terms of competition), or severe climate change (in terms of technological progress or a shift in the unpredictable habits of consumers.)

These kinds of environmental changes can happen in a number of ways: *gradually,* as a result of numerous alterations in the ecosystem, or *suddenly,* as a result of a cataclysmic shock. Either way, the analogy isn't pretty. Scientists are divided as to what killed the dinosaurs. Some believe it was creeping climate change, a cooling off of the environment due to volcanic activity and slow shifts in the continental plates. Others believe it was the sudden impact of an asteroid. But even under that theory, asteroids didn't just hit the dinosaurs in the head. Rather, they whacked Earth so forcefully that they dislodged poisonous soot into the atmosphere, trapping acid rain, cutting off sunlight, and bringing on the equivalent of a nuclear winter.

What could set off equivalent changes on the World Wide Web? There are numerous possibilities. The most obvious is that stockholders suddenly will cut and run, finally recognizing that certain much-touted business models really don't work or rediscovering that *profits* are what makes corporations valuable—not just revenue alone, not hits, not page views, not mentions in press, not the buzz among financial analysts, not the amount of free shrimp offered at trade show events. And we're talking real profits. Not profits before "special one-time charges." Not profits excluding special write-offs for acquisitions. Not profits before this or that accounting trick. But net income. Earnings per share. Sooner or later the bottom line will end up being the bottom line.

If brontosaurian market valuations fall to comprehensible levels, the venture capital pipeline backs up: If the rewards at the end aren't as spectacular, then investors will be more selective. And if fewer firms can go public with success, the most attractive exit strategy for the venture capitalist is no longer available. Massive investments could be lost, future investments could dry up, and there wouldn't be new manna from heaven to sustain new lifeforms. In certain quarters this has already started happening. "The next wave," says one venture capitalist, "is going to be a lot different." Darwin put it another way: "We forget that though food may be now superabundant, it is not so at all seasons of each recurring year."

An even more likely scenario is this one: Perhaps the dinosaurs in this metaphor are really the gigantic transnational corporations that have ruled over their respective industries for virtual eons. Perhaps the formation of the Web itself is the cataclysmic event in a much larger evolutionary scheme. Perhaps the global auto giants, the megabanks, the bigfoot telephone companies, the media conglomerates, the consumer product colossi, the finance and insurance amalgamations, the protected species of utilities, and the sprawling retail behemoths are the ones in danger of extinction. Or perhaps a few have enough smarts to adapt into something far more flexible, responsive, and innovative. Remarkably, this too has already started happening.

Technological change itself will play a big role in determining the fate of these corporate species. The most important shift will be in the gradual adoption of high-speed, multimegabit access over cable modems and digital phone lines. Flashing, pulsating bits of light will be racing more rapidly through strands of fiber. If there is no cumbersome dial-up process, the Internet will always be "on."

Just before the turn of the century, only about 1 percent of U.S.

households with Internet access had high-speed data lines. That figure could grow to 20 percent or more over the next several years if access fees are based on reasonable, flat monthly rates. So, as it becomes far faster to look something up online, as it becomes far more convenient to perform a transaction online than it is to do it elsewhere, then people will simply use the Web for more and more tasks. As Web commerce becomes easier and cheaper, it will touch more and more areas of life.

The shifting habits of consumers also play a big part in environmental change. As time passes, habits form, aimless surfing decreases, and people naturally become even more and more selective as to how they spend their finite attention. Studies show that the longer consumers have been online, the more likely they are to be performing transactions. More than 40 percent of those with more than four years of experience online are regularly shopping online and conducting Web commerce, as opposed to 12 percent of those who have been online for less than a year. Yet as the molten lava of surfing and experimentation hardens into encrusted, trusted loyalties, as the Web becomes more useful to more people, more and more companies will enter these digital markets, and competition will become more and more brutal.

Perhaps the most dramatic arena for competition will be staged among the search engines, the Web navigation sites. Darwin is already alive and well among the so-called portals. The top nine portals—those of Alta Vista, America Online, Excite, Infoseek, Lycos, Microsoft, Netscape, Snap, and Yahoo—have in recent years accounted for a mere 15 percent of all Internet traffic. Yet they have attracted about 60 percent of all advertising spending on the Web. They are, in effect, taking in four times more revenue than they are worth. The top five U.S. television networks, by contrast, attract 67 percent of all viewers and take in a more reasonable 84 percent of TV advertising.

Advertising spending on the Web is not all that big a source of sustenance—only a couple billion dollars annually—especially when compared to the vastly greater e-commerce opportunity. As these overvalued, overrated digital media enterprises fight over this rather modest market, competition could get barbarous and consolidation more rapid. We've already seen some of this, with AOL buying Netscape and bigger companies such as GE/NBC, Disney, and Compaq investing in Snap, Infoseek, and Alta Vista, respectively.

But these early skirmishes are only a hint of what's to come. "The struggle will almost invariably be most severe between the individuals of the same species," warned Darwin, "for they frequent the same districts, require the same food, and are exposed to the same dangers."

"This is natural Darwinism," says Tim Koogle, the CEO of Yahoo. And the dangers are very real, he says. "There are lots of companies on the Web," adds Koogle, "but there aren't very many businesses." He's right, of course. But that's pretty easy for him to say. Perhaps the greatest thing about Yahoo's business model, its secret competitive advantage, is that it doesn't have to burn piles of cash each month advertising, well, on Yahoo.

The online retail landscape is evolving in a similarly Darwinian fashion. Mary Meeker, the influential Morgan Stanley analyst, outlines a theory she calls "the Wal-Marting of the Web." In her research report, she has a chart showing that before Wal-Mart, there are five stores in a typical small town: a record store, a shoe store, an appliance store, a five-and-dime, and a clothing store. Those stores, in this scenario, represent 100 percent of the retail marketplace in town. After Wal-Mart shows up, all of those stores are out of business and Wal-Mart has 100 percent of the marketplace.

"The Web is one big small town," Meeker writes. "Whether a user is in Shanghai, New York, or Peoria, they can shop at the same store. Within five years, the Web should obtain from 1% to 4% of global retail spending. We should see super-consolidation with a few winners. Who needs thousands of bookstores?" Meeker points out that it's not just low prices but the efficient inventory and distribution systems that enable the winners to manage costs better.

But if you follow this line of thought, it becomes quite grim. It's a zero-sum theory. It has no built-in value-added component, just a shift in sales from one source to another. A more likely scenario is that the Amazon.coms of the Web economy become hybrid companies, a little like Wal-Mart, yes, but also a lot like Microsoft. Whether you believe Microsoft is a predatory monopolist is beside the point. Unlike Wal-Mart, which has simply been successful at shifting other people's sales into its own pockets, Microsoft helped create from scratch an entirely new industry—the software and intellectual property industry—that has accounted for so much of the upsurge in the world economy over latter part of the twentieth century. By many accounts, 30 percent of all recent economic growth in the United States is due to information technology.

As a universe of intellectual property, the Web represents the ultimate forum for constant innovation. As we'll see, offering the lowest prices and becoming the most efficient supplier of goods and services is not nearly enough. The only way to differentiate your Web venture is by creating new value-added applications, assembling bundles of information, and inventing interactive services that transform mere transactions into unique, personalized experiences that competitors would have a tough time replicating.

Here's the question: Is the Web (A) just another place for doing the same old things in just a slightly different setting? Or (B) does it permit people to do new things and let companies add unique, new improvements to old things? The answer has to be B if the Web economy is to continue to expand in all directions.

The Grand Unification

Since the Web is a personal, interactive medium, one in which each user's experience is unique, it will never be adept at creating mass exposure or awareness for your product, company, or brand. Yes, the Web can work in concert with mass media to build your business, but it will never become like television as we have known it. Instead, the Web can deliver something more powerful that other media cannot: tangible results. Completed transactions. Lower costs. Loyal customers.

In the hopelessly cluttered Web marketplace, trusted brands are more important than ever, and companies must never undermine that trust. Lasting relationships with consumers and business partners are built on the exchange of information. Customers will gladly disclose data about themselves provided that they get something valuable in return, such as personal service, product discounts, or free information and advice. Companies can make money by protecting the privacy of their customers, not by violating it.

People will shop online but only for "information-rich" products and services that are worth the time and effort to spend researching. When doing so, self-service provides for the ultimate in customer comfort. That is a huge benefit to companies that aim to reduce costs and boost customer satisfaction at the same time. Even the smallest players can expand globally provided that they customize their content for certain cultures. And finally—perhaps most important—successful Web enterprises must move fast and constantly innovate.

The evolution of technology won't alter those basic principles of Webonomics. Rather, these principles form the foundation for developing new, more sophisticated survival strategies. For instance, the Web economy of the past has been approached by users, companies, and investors as if it existed in its own parallel universe. Yet one thing is quite clear: We of the Web are not alone. We must recognize that the Web is coevolving and coadapting along with the greater world of business and culture around it.

Indeed, life on the Web becomes exponentially richer when it is tightly integrated with the familiar physical world. Thus the companies that use both mass media and interactive media to reinforce one another will be among the most successful. The companies that integrate Web commerce with all their other channels of business will be among those that create the most wealth. We do not need a Wal-Mart of the Web. Rather, we need the Web to do what cannot be accomplished elsewhere.

Yet even as they intertwine with one another, the online realm will still differ profoundly from the physical one. There is no geography on the Web. Despite the many offers that users receive by junk e-mail to sell them valuable online real estate, tony domain addresses, and plots of the Web's beachfront property, the mantra of location, location, location doesn't apply to the Web. Real estate is based on scarcity, and Web terrain is infinite. One website is more valuable than another because of the value associated with its brand, not its location—its properties, not its property.

The process of cross-pollinating and cross-breeding these two very different worlds will no doubt create some interesting and powerful hybrids. This book ends up presenting a unification strategy, an approach that can be called real-world integration. Along the way there, we'll discover other essential survival strategies that demonstrate how the Web is conducive to new forms of branding, pricing, marketing, packaging, manufacturing, and adding new value to transactions between buyers and sellers.

Taken together, the strategies that follow will show that the Web is more than a new landscape for doing business, more than a digital terrain that leads to brand-new species of companies. The frenetic evolution we are undergoing will forever alter the way *all* business is conducted almost everywhere by almost everyone. The purpose of this book is to act as a survival guide for executives at companies at every level of digital evolution, with the hope that readers will gain an imposing advantage in the grand struggle for existence.

BUILD A BRAND THAT STANDS FOR SOLVING PROBLEMS

The Quest for a Solution Brand

Anyone can sell products cheaply on the Web. But your company won't survive unless you do much more than that. You must evolve into a problem solver, identifying a specific set of issues that your customers face, then developing a set of interactive services that address those problems. In doing so, you can create a strong "solution brand" that can serve as a fortress against enemy invasion.

Let's start with one of the most intractable and nagging problems that people face: shopping for groceries. Every family needs groceries, yet surveys always show that the vast majority of people consider such shopping repetitive, time consuming, and, most of the time, fairly dreadful. The race to provide the best online grocery shopping and delivery service has been both fascinating and frustrating. And it's shaping up to be an epic quest for the ultimate solution brand.

The story begins with Peapod Inc., the Skokie, Illinois, company that has been trying to turn a profit selling groceries online for more than ten years now. Founded by Andrew Parkinson, a former Procter & Gamble manager of such high-profile brands as Pringles, Duncan Hines, and Parkay, along with his younger brother Thomas, a software designer, Peapod began delivering groceries in the Chicago area and then expanded to San Francisco, Houston, Dallas, Austin, Boston, Atlanta, and other regions filled with high-tech, high-income, time-crunched people. By its 10-year anniversary in 1999, more than 100,000 households were ordering through the service, and Peapod was posting annual revenue of close to $100 million.

Peapod built the country's most well-known online grocery brand through local advertising, attracting press coverage, and sending out America Online–type blast mailings of millions of free sign-up diskettes to potential customers in its target metro areas. Its tag line (America's Internet Grocer) and its slogan ("Smart Shopping for Busy People") seem to say exactly what it is and does. Yet despite its name recognition, its market value and overall financial performance have been immensely disappointing. *Barron's,* in 1997, honored Peapod with the distinction of being the worst-performing Web-related initial public offering (IPO) of the year.

Why? First off, Peapod has been stuck from the start in partnerships with real grocery chains that own expensive real estate—multibillion-dollar giants such as Stop & Shop, Safeway, and Kroger. As a result, Peapod is not the one making money from buying the food wholesale and selling it retail. In each local market, consumers transmit their orders over the Web, then Peapod personnel gather the food from local supermarket shelves, which are three times more expensive to stock and maintain as central warehouses located in industrial areas. The company has begun building such warehouses, enabling Peapod to "pick and pack up to five times faster," says Andrew Parkinson. But that reduces its costs only somewhat and doesn't change the fact that Peapod is ultimately just a delivery boy for the big supermarket chains. It makes its money charging subscription fees (usually $4.95 per month) and per-delivery charges (typically $5 per order).

As Peapod has grown, signing up more and more households in more markets, this business model has become a near-perfect paradox. "The more successful they are, the more money they lose," quips Ryan Mathews, a former editor of *Progressive Grocer* and now an industry consultant. In a recent four-year period, net losses have increased every year, for a terrifying total of more than $45 million in red ink over that time.

In addition, Peapod seems to have lost sight of what its main mission should be: providing the ultimate life-simplifying solution to its customers. Since it has been struggling to find a way to make money from delivering groceries, it has turned much of its attention back to the makers of the products it sells rather than keeping focused on the people it's serving. Every click, every purchase, every online move a consumer makes on the Peapod service is captured into databases. The information is sold back to the P&Gs, Krafts, and Unilevers of the world.

The elder Parkinson explains that the manufacturers are interested in the process of how a consumer moves through a store—which products they click on but do not put in their virtual shopping baskets, whether they look up the nutritional information, whether they sort by price and pick the lowest one, or whether they always buy the same brands no matter what the price. "We're creating a medium for packaged goods companies . . . a research learning vehicle," says Parkinson. He expects to obtain the majority of any future profits from those corporations, not from consumers.

Yes, Peapod had an interesting idea: automated grocery shopping. But it hasn't been able to look well beyond groceries and attack the much deeper problem of helping people manage a wide range of daily household chores. Perhaps the biggest shortcoming is that customers in many regions it serves must be home to accept delivery. When placing an order, they select a three-hour time window the next day. But waiting at home for the delivery doesn't enable the time-saving or time-shifting that busy people want.

The very name Peapod suggests a focus on the food—that the consumer's perishables will arrive as green and crisp as peapods. Even the company's ads underscore this: A chipper Peapod delivery boy is pictured walking up a driveway carrying bags bursting with fresh vegetables. But the brand shouldn't be about the food. It should be about solving the core problem at hand.

A Technology Fixation

Perhaps the problem with Peapod's business is that it actually goes to the trouble of *delivering* the groceries.

That, at least, was the view of Daniel Nissan, founder of a New York–based start-up called NetGrocer Inc., which began offering a selection of thousands of grocery and drugstore items from its website. Nissan, an Israeli from Tel Aviv, was an executive at the Internet telephony start-up VocalTech before he started this new company, at age 30, back in 1996.

One of many entrepreneurs who believed that the grocery store of the future will exist on your home computer, Nissan laid claim to the inside track to profitability in this brutally competitive business. Peapod, Nissan notes, has its own fleet of more than 1,000 delivery vans. This necessitates paying drivers and delivery people, buying or leasing the vans, purchasing gas, paying insurance premiums, and worrying about driver liability. "It's impossible to make money doing that," he says.

By contrast, NetGrocer ships to anywhere in the continental United States—centrally from a New Jersey–based food warehouse the size of a football field. As a result, it has become the first truly national online store offering a wide selection of groceries. To accomplish this, NetGrocer simply outsources the package delivery to a company that specializes in it: FedEx, which delivers the orders within two to three days. There are no monthly charges for using NetGrocer, but shipping charges have been a flat $2.99 if the order is below 50 pounds and $4.99 if it's above. (The average order costs $70 and weighs 48 pounds.) Since those shipping charges are only a small portion of what NetGrocer must pay to FedEx, the company has had to take a loss on the shipping and try to make it up in food volume.

It may sound absurd to FedEx diapers, canned soup, paper towels, laundry detergent, and peanut butter and jelly. But Nissan believes that online shoppers will want the convenience of having these nonperishable, pantry items delivered at low cost while choosing to buy their fruits, vegetables, meats, and other perishables in person at local specialty shops.

Nissan already has observed this shopping split in nearby New York neighborhoods, as he watches shoppers enter D'Agostino's, a general grocery store, to buy pantry items and then continue on to Fairway or Zabar's to buy meats, fresh vegetables, and specialty foods. "We want to replace the D'Agostino's of the world," Nissan says. That's the solution people are looking for, he believes. People want to continue shopping in person for the more interesting items and have their boring, mundane pantry staples arrive as if they were on a monthly subscription.

Yet even under this very different model, turning a profit will be tricky. Managing the costs is only half the battle. "What you can't manage is the increasing expectations of consumers," says Mathews, the food industry consultant. "After a while, you're not dazzling me by getting me a can of Spaghettios in two or three days. Pretty soon people will want it the next day."

And this leads to another big question: Are you really offering a solution if the solution is only partial? Many consumers want all of their food delivered, not just dry goods. The top item ordered on Peapod, for instance, is bananas.

When NetGrocer tried to go public in the fall of 1998, it had to disclose the fact that it was losing a whopping $1 million every month and only collecting a paltry $136,000 in monthly revenue. Another eye-opener: To get people to its front door, it had signed deals to make fixed payments totaling $16 million to AOL, Yahoo, Excite, and iVillage over the next year. That the company was one-third owned by Cendant Corp., then in the news for massive accounting fraud, didn't exactly help either.

You don't need to blame any temporary bear market in IPOs for the fact that investors turned ugly on this deal. The stock offering was quietly withdrawn. Cendant took another embarrassing accounting write-off, this one for $50 million, and the board of directors ended up ousting Nissan and replacing him with a new CEO.

Whereas Peapod focused on the products, NetGrocer was fixated on the technology. The very name of the company suggests that the Internet will somehow make grocery shopping better. All of the company's promotional materials touted it as "the first online nationwide supermarket" and "the premier electronic grocery store on the Web," but they said very little about the customer experience. As a result, NetGrocer was really a technology brand, not a solution brand.

Zeroing in on the Problem

Timothy DeMello took a different approach: Instead of setting out to sell groceries over the Internet, first he went about finding out exactly what customers needed. Born and educated in the affluent suburbs of Boston, DeMello is a former college baseball player turned stockbroker turned entrepreneur. He has neatly trimmed brown hair and a manic but affable personality. He began studying the way busy suburban families went about their daily routines.

"Consumers have been taking the things they need to do and the things they want to do and making one big to-do list," he says. "In my opinion, they would rather separate the two and outsource the stuff that isn't necessarily enjoyable to someone else. Time is the commodity we should be selling. We should be creating a brand that will simplify people's lives."

That brand turned into something called Streamline. DeMello founded the company at age 34 in 1993, just before use of the Web exploded. The Web, he says, wasn't the *driver* behind the company, it was the *enabler*. The problem he wanted to solve will exist regardless of changes in the technology. But, he says, the company wouldn't have been able to do what it has been doing without the Web.

For three years, DeMello studied his very specific target market, drew up business plans, and raised money. He invested $45,000 of his own cash to pay for office space and raised $1.7 million from numerous friends, family members, and colleagues. He used the cash to build a 65,000-square-foot grocery distribution center in Westwood, Massachusetts, near Route 128.

"I really didn't know what I was doing," he now admits. When he pitched his business plan to one well-connected New York investor, offering him 40 percent ownership in the young company in return for $5 million, the investor agreed on the spot. "I knew right then that I had made a mistake," he says, referring to the classic entrepreneurial error of handing over too much equity too soon.

DeMello started by signing up 100 households in the area to test his new service. This is how it works: Representatives from the company come to your house and take inventory, going through pantries and refrigerators with a bar-code scanner. From this they create a custom shopping list for your online account. Then you begin shopping on Streamline's website, choosing from among tens of thousands of grocery products. Since it keeps track of the products you like, if you click on "tuna" on your list, it already knows to deliver 16-ounce cans of Bumble Bee. One feature, called DRO, for "don't run out," will automatically add a new packet of, say, razor blades to your shopping basket when it knows you are about to finish your old ones.

Streamline began adding more and more services to the online menu. In addition to groceries and drugstore items, its uniformed delivery people will pick up and return your Blockbuster videos; take care of your dry cleaning, film development, prescription refills, shoe repairs, and post office trips; plus a half-dozen or so other common chores. The aim is to increase how much each household spends, not necessarily to enroll as many households as possible. "We're focused on increasing our share of customer," he says, "not our share of market."

Families pay $30 per month to subscribe to Streamline. The subscription fee includes the installation of a special, refrigerated "smart box" that is attached to the side of your house or sits in your basement or garage—essentially a larger version of the old-fashioned milk box. With the smart box, the family doesn't have to be home when the Streamline delivery van arrives. True time-shifting can occur.

Within two years, nearly 2,000 families signed up, each getting deliveries an average of 46 times per year and spending an average of nearly $6,000 annually, with many going as high as $12,000. (By contrast, Peapod's average customer spends less than $1,000 per year; NetGrocer's even less.) Streamline was now serving nearly 5 percent of the households in some of these Boston suburbs, and the company was getting closer and closer to turning a profit.

The time was right to start expanding. DeMello went out and raised $10 million from investors such as Intel, PaineWebber, and G.E. Capital, the firm that also owns and manages Streamline's fleet of delivery vans. Then the Nordstrom department store chain kicked in another $23 million. Nordstrom, the longtime business school textbook case study in responsive service, saw this as the ultimate in customer intimacy and in loyalty marketing, so it wanted in on the action.

Intel engineers developed some new whiz-bang software for the Streamline service. Instead of just viewing an image of the cereal box, customers could click on a 3-D image, and it flips around to the back. Instead of just ordering bananas, they could view different gradations of ripeness and click on the shade of yellow or green that they wanted. They could choose from a file of recipes (such as honey nut bread) or entire meals (such as lasagna), specify the serving size, have all the necessary ingredients appear on screen, and click on the items they required.

While DeMello's goal is to make this a process that only takes up to 22 minutes once per week, some people choose to use it for longer periods of time because of the incredible variety of services offered. Customers take advantage of new features such as the ability to view online images of photos they have sent for developing, then e-mail copies to friends and family members.

Beginning with a foray into the affluent Washington, D.C., suburbs in Maryland and Virginia, DeMello has set out on a seven-year expansion plan. He wants to ramp up to a total of 150 warehouses serving the 20 top geographic markets in the United States. Each distribution center should require up to two dozen new vans, up to 250 employees, serve up to 8,000 households, and bring in perhaps $50 million in revenue apiece, he says. But he expects the demographic to remain the same: 90 percent of customers have kids, half the families are single income and half are dual, with average household earnings averaging about $100,000. Really wealthy people aren't in the target market because they already have a household chores solution: It's called domestic staff.

Changing Consumer Habits

Competition in the online grocery market has been especially Darwinian because of the towering expectations that consumers hold for such services. For centuries people have been going out into the marketplace and gathering their foodstuffs. If a new digital service is going to replace this timeworn ritual, it has to pass an especially rigorous fitness test. The unfit ones will simply die off.

Currently, less than 1 percent of U.S. households order groceries online. But Andersen Consulting forecasts that the online ordering model will account for 10 to 15 percent of the $400 billion–plus grocery and household consumer goods industry by 2007, a projection with which others agree. And so the opportunity is huge: This market is much greater than the one for books and recorded music combined, just to name two popular e-commerce categories that have caught on more quickly.

In a sense, the home delivery model is a back-to-the-future strategy, as grocery delivery boys were a common option before the rise of mega-supermarkets over the past 40 or so years. If it can be resurrected and made more efficient on the Web, this model may skim off the most profitable portion of the shopping population. "Even if it's only 10 percent of the population shopping online, every indication is that it's the 10 percent most profitable customers, and they account for up to 40 percent of the industry's profits," says consultant Mathews. "This could cripple the big supermarkets."

Yet none of the founders of Peapod, NetGrocer, or Streamline think that this will make all local retail obsolete. DeMello, for one, expects that people will still go to the local butcher for special cuts of meat and still saunter into fresh produce stands and still frequent the local coffeeshop, the local bookstore, and other small specialty shops. But they'll do this because they enjoy going to these Main Street–type places, he says, not because they have to.

Many consumers have absolutely no intention of giving up their mundane chores. Even though we *can* eliminate them, such tasks can be viewed as an integral part of life, and performing them confers a certain dignity. The split may very well be generational. "My daughter learned to write her name on a Macintosh when she was three," says Mathews. "I can't imagine that, as an adult, she will be lugging home Tide from the supermarket."

So for those who are more than willing to make the switch, the brands that stand the best chance of being relevant are the ones that offer overarching solutions, the ones that help people simplify their lives by organizing their time better. The lesson: Don't offer a brand focused around products (Peapod) or around technology (NetGrocer). Offer one that embraces consumers and tells them how much better their daily life will be. "Your brand," says DeMello, "is your promise to the customer." That promise must be as large as the problem that you are trying to alleviate. And the companies that deliver on that bold promise will no doubt enjoy a long, prosperous existence.

Why Web Branding Is Different

Brands may not be what you think they are. Brands don't exist on store shelves, in TV commercials, or even on websites. They exist solely in the minds of consumers, making brand strategy a form of psychological warfare. Branding is also about far more than awareness. Like a neglected house, some world-famous brands that everyone knows can fall into a state of disrepair (remember what happened to Woolworth's), while some of the world's strongest brands don't even ring a bell with most people (such as Callaway golf clubs, the Rolls-Royce of golf equipment).

A brand isn't just a famous name. Says Stuart Agres, a top executive with global advertising powerhouse Young & Rubicam (Y&R): "A brand is a set of differentiating promises that link a product or a service to its customers."

Today's concept of branding has been built up in stages over time. It all began in ancient Egypt when shepherds started putting name tags on their livestock. ("Hello, my name is Omar the Ibex. If found, please return me to Achmed.") Shepherds thus became the world's first-known brands. The practice of branding livestock endured, eventually spreading to the early American West, which was overrun with wild cattle. Using a branding iron to burnish a badge on a bull's behind became a prime pastime of Texas cattle culture. Cattle ranch brands such as Alamo and Austin became known throughout the land as symbols of ownership, pride, and prestige.

A more sophisticated use of branding developed in medieval Europe. Plagues were a major ordeal at the time, and people were becoming ill from drinking brews infested with germs and nasty vermin. The German purity law of 1516 was a hugely successful attempt to change that. And so beer brands sprang up to tell the drinker that these lagers were brewed in accordance with the regulation. From then on, brands were used to confer quality. And people would pay more if they were assured higher quality.

Or some other sort of distinct attribute. Following the lead of the German brewers, whiskey distillers began shipping their concoctions all over the known world—in wooden barrels with the producer's name burned onto them. In 1835 a band of bootleggers introduced Old Smuggler, a brand of Scotch made using a special distillation process. Branding now had a new role: product differentiation as well as ownership and quality.

Initially these attributes had to travel largely by word of mouth, as mass media hadn't yet evolved. When mass-circulation newspapers appeared in the late 1800s, several companies seized the opportunity and introduced national advertisements. The first national, multimillion-dollar advertising campaign was for Nabisco's Uneeda Biscuits in 1889. Other early national brands included Prudential's life insurance and Procter & Gamble's Ivory Soap ("It floats!" and "99 and 44/100% pure" became their points of differentiation.) Mass marketing had begun, and branding was its most potent tool. By 1922, according to Webster's, "brand name" was accepted as an adjective, as in "brand-name car" or "brand-name cracker."

With the advent of radio and then television, branding became somewhat of a weird science and a black art at the same time. But if you think about many of the dominant brands established in the mass media, they are different from the most valuable brands established on the Web. To understand why, we have to go back to a distinction introduced in my earlier book, *Webonomics*:

> The distinguishing factor between one-way media and two-way, or interactive media, is the simple matter of control. In traditional media, advertising is *intrusive.* The marketer purchases space and has complete control over what goes in that space. The viewer or reader has to look at that ad as the marketer intended it. The only recourse is turning the page or changing the channel. As a result, the advertisers can say whatever they want. And they sometimes take this paid-for privilege to absurd heights. Does anybody honestly believe, for instance, that drinking Slim-Fast shakes twice a day amounts to "balanced nutrition for a healthy life," as the company's slogan says? Probably not. But if you repeat it often enough using an *emotional* rather than a *rational* appeal, you end up with a brand image.

Rational branding has become a new buzzword among Web marketers. "Rational branding strives both to move and to help the online consumer at the same time," says *BusinessWeek* in an article on the topic. "But the tactic poses a real challenge to makers of consumer products. There are frighteningly few ways to make soap or soda useful in the virtual world. Indeed, of the top five buyers in TV advertising, most are nearly invisible online."

It's indeed telling that no new soft drinks or beers, no new soaps and detergents, no new cereals or frozen entrees, no new makes of cars and trucks have established new brands solely on the Web. Consider brands such as Tide detergent, AT&T long distance, Disney films, Ford trucks, Miller beer, Kellogg's cereals, Coca-Cola, and so on. Yes, they are all products and services with famous, valuable brand names. The makers of these products typically spend hundreds of millions of dollars, if not billions, every year on ads that try to differentiate their offerings from competing ones. Yes, Coke will quench your thirst and Tide will clean your clothes. But none is really aimed at intricate multistep problem domains, as are many of the emerging brands on the Web. These mass media brands were created to solve the problems of sellers, not consumers.

Products such as Coke and Tide use emotion to try to forge identity. And on the Web, consumers do not have to endure emotion-laden advertisements. They spend their time doing things, finding things, getting chores done—and sidestepping ads. The most valuable Web brands—including Yahoo, Amazon.com, and E*Trade—are not product brands. They are brands for a complex set of services—solutions—that help people cut through the clutter and perform a series of tasks.

"Consumers are not looking for more choice," says Mark Dempster, director of brand strategy for USWeb/CKS, a Silicon Valley marketing strategy agency. They have enough product choice already. "Rather, they are looking for 'made-for-me' solutions." Unlike mass media, the interactive, personal media such as the Web simply aren't good at burnishing an emotionally charged message into the minds of millions. The Web is adept at taking a user through a series of screens, a step-by-step process with an end result in mind. Consumers actually use the Web as a tool to accomplish a particular objective.

Solution branding may not be entirely new. (High-tech service firms, from IBM to EDS, are among those that have been touting for years the idea that "We sell solutions.") What *is* new is the rise of interactive solution services and how the new brands in this domain are already beginning to rival the prestige of the venerable mass-media brands.

What Makes for a Strong Brand?

Still, Web-based businesses can learn a lot from the past. Emotion-based product brands such as Coke and Pepsi have showed the world that if branding isn't everything, it's sure damn close. Countless studies have shown that there's nothing like a strong brand for juicing both your net income and stock price. Coca-Cola's brand names, for instance, are worth a staggering $167 billion (the difference between its physical assets of $15 billion and its recent stock market capitalization of $182 billion). Such brand equity is no doubt one of the most stunning achievements in modern business. By repeating the emotional attributes and sheer sensibilities of sweetened fizzy water enough times in advertisements and promotions, Coke has become the world's most ubiquitous brand.

Many of the same tactics and techniques pioneered by the product brands we all know transcend media and are still critical for creating these new solution brands. According to Y&R, the process of building any strong brand must begin with *brand differentiation,* which is "the perceived distinctiveness" of the product or service. "Differentiation gives birth to the brand," says Y&R's Agres, who leads an ongoing research project called the Brand

Asset Valuator, an assessment of 8,500 brands that involves interviewing tens of thousands of consumers in 24 countries.

The first question that emerging Internet businesses need to ask is: "What makes this brand stand apart?" Coca-Cola and Disney, for instance, still maintain their differentiation—that is, they have been adept at demonstrating what their products are about and identifying and attaching new attributes to themselves. By contrast, TWA and Greyhound—brands that are declining in distinctiveness—do not, according to the study. Among Web brands, CDnow and Music Boulevard seemed to struggle to stand apart from one another, thus explaining, in part, why they rushed into each other's arms and merged. No one seemed to know why one online music store was better or worse than the other.

The second pillar of building brand equity is establishing *brand relevance*. Customers are always subconsciously asking: "Does this brand speak to me?" This is the so-called personal appropriateness of the brand. You can be extremely aware of what a brand stands for without being personally interested in making the brand a part of your life. Think of Ferrari and Victoria's Secret. Many people know exactly what makes these brands different, yet they address the real needs of only a certain few. You can become a market leader with high differentiation and low relevance, but ultimately your product will reach a very targeted market. On the flip side, you can be relevant to many people but not differentiated. Witness the dozens of low-cost online stock brokerage services on the Web that have failed to establish leadership in their category. The trick is to make your brand relevant to as many people as possible without losing your differentiation.

The third factor is *brand esteem,* which is a measure of how highly consumers regard the brand. This is closely related to perceived quality or feelings of popularity on the part of consumers. Global brands with the highest esteem ratings due to perceived quality include Hallmark and Kodak. Those with high esteem ratings due to a widespread sense of popularity or trendiness—brands that are perhaps not as evolved—may include Yahoo and Amazon.com.

Finally, the fourth factor, *brand knowledge,* measures the consumer's understanding of the brand's inner workings. High brand knowledge suggests acute customer intimacy or proof that consumers are experienced with how your product or service works for them—for better and for worse. Y&R considers this the culmination of any branding effort.

Yes, strong brands need both high esteem and knowledge. Brands with high knowledge and low esteem tend to be desperately discounting their products to avoid losing market share or serving a market with polarized opinion about them. People may know a lot about them but not hold a high opinion of them. Examples of such brands, according to the Y&R study, include McDonald's and the National Rifle Association.

Conversely, brands with high esteem and low knowledge tend to be newer, expanding, and possessing some sort of unrealized potential. That's the perfect description for many of the newer Web brands. The danger, of course, is that these names can take on the aura of a passing fad. "Consumers want to be seen going with the winner," says Agres. But if the perceived popularity drops, if the fad fades, then there is nothing left propping it up. That's why brands that only have esteem going for them and neglect the other three pillars can be in grave danger.

Although the Brand Asset Valuator was developed originally to measure mass-media brands names, these four pillars of building brand equity also apply to the millions of domain names in the emerging Web economy. And most Web-based brands have yet to take the leap into this more sophisticated realm of thinking. As a result, many young companies make the mistake of equating brand strength with simplistic awareness, a mistake that may lead to brand death.

"The battle can't solely be for people's attention," Agres says. It's not just about people knowing your name, but what your name stands for, whether it speaks to people's real needs, whether people hold it in high regard, and whether your promises are delivered upon when consumers finally have real, firsthand experience with it. In general, he says, growing, thriving, profitable brands should have higher ratings for differentiation than relevance and higher ratings for esteem than knowledge.

Solution brands have to leap especially high barriers en route to these goals. Let's bring it back to the online grocery services. "It shouldn't just be online retail," Agres concludes. "Online retail is besides the point. It has to be more than the superficial we'll-deliver-your-groceries message. It has to be: What is the brand doing for me? How do I benefit? Communicate the promise." And deliver the promise as well as the groceries.

Keeping Your Solution Brand Alive

Brands exist in a larger, overall context, which is constantly shifting. The surrounding environment comprises many elements, including the changing expectations of customers, what your competitors are doing, how investors perceive your market segment, and new technological developments.

The fact that the larger market conditions can mutate unexpectedly is well known in the traditional world of branding. "The sands constantly shift," says Mark Dempster, the USWeb/CKS brand strategist. "CEOs that don't pay attention will have the context of their brand change right under them."

As a result, brands that seem dominant one minute can lose their footing the next. And on the Web, that can happen by the next time you upgrade your browser. The Netscape brand name, for instance, was practically synonymous with the Web's early, we've-just-discovered-a-new-planet sensibility. Customers, competitors, and investors were euphoric over it. It exhibited enormously high differentiation and esteem.

Then the context shifted. "When we started Netscape, we thought we were a software company," says cofounder Marc Andreessen, the chief developer of the first commercial Web browser. "What do software companies do? They create software and sell it. Turns out, that's not the business model that made sense for us. People already have more software than they know what to do with, and we had to keep giving away the software just to get people to use it." Obviously, with Microsoft's entrance into Netscape's core market, the competitive landscape was altered enormously and permanently.

Netscape's business then shifted toward selling software for corporate intranets. Consumers might not pay for browser software, they thought, but corporations would pay for industrial-strength network management software and related services. This new sector rapidly became the company's biggest source of revenue. But as Netscape was battling Microsoft in those markets too and concentrating on corporate software, the context was mutating yet again.

Yahoo and other Web search services were paying Netscape about $5 million per year for choice spots on its home page, which happened to be the default home page for tens of millions of Web surfers worldwide. Directed properly, the attention of these people was worth far more than that. Yahoo parlayed that aggregation of attention into a market valuation topping $20 billion, while Netscape's market value was stagnating. By early 1998 Netscape was forced to shift its focus to take advantage of this key opportunity, this time to developing its NetCenter home page into a major "portal," a navigation service that tries to cut through the choice and complexity for the user. Netscape was now in competition with one of its main business partners.

But Netscape's portal lacked differentiation. While Yahoo was evolving its Web experience brand in many new ways, Netscape was forced into a perpetual game of catch-up. By the time it was swallowed by America Online, Netscape's NetCenter had plenty of traffic, but it trailed that of Yahoo. And more important, it offered little in the way of unique solutions or features. Its stock market valuation and corporate behavior reflected that.

Toward the end of its existence as an independent entity, Netscape was lashing out ferociously at its competitors, sometimes in defensive terror. It finally fetched $4.2 billion—approximately the same valuation that it had shortly after going public three years earlier. In an e-mail message unearthed in the landmark government trial against Microsoft, Netscape's Andreessen urged America Online chairman Steve Case to combine forces against a larger predator. "We must use our unique strengths to kick the [expletive] out of the Beast from Redmond that wants to see us both dead," Andreessen wrote.

The longer you let your brand drift and the longer you let your competitors define what the new context is, the harder it becomes to reposition the brand in the new context. This is true across every industry.

The Howard Johnson's hotel chain is another case in point. "HoJo is a venerable brand that has gone stale," Dempster says. "You think of those wonderful family car trips in a station wagon in the 1950s and 1960s. But it has lost its footing in an age when Hyatt and Hilton have become more like high-tech corporate offices than hotels." The entire context of what a hotel should be had been transformed. But HoJo's properties and image were still the same. It had high brand knowledge and low esteem. Everyone seemed to know and understand the brand, but they didn't think too highly of it compared to its competitors.

These days the top manager of the HoJo brand happens to be Wall Street financial whiz Henry Silverman, the CEO of marketing giant Cendant. Silverman had purchased HoJo along with Ramada (another high-knowledge, low-esteem brand) for $170 million in the early 1990s, then proceeded to kick 150 hotels out of the Howard Johnson's system. He also forced others to upgrade their facilities and quality of service—all aimed at rebuilding brand esteem. But whether he succeeds in reconnecting consumers with HoJo, creating a new promise for the brand, remains to be seen.

Rebuilding such a brand, according to David Aaker, a brand strategy expert at University of California at Berkeley, is usually a long, tough slog. "Schlitz Beer tried to rebuild its brand and failed," Aaker says. "Toyota and Nissan did it, but it took them 15 years." In the new Web economy, no one has that kind of time. "The brand manager of the future is like an air traffic controller," Dempster says. "It's all happening in real time."

Shift happens! That's why Yahoo doesn't just react to but actively goes about causing such shifts. As a result, Yahoo often seems as if it is a solution brand that is constantly in frantic search of new problems to solve. It seems to be reinventing its brand every 90 days. The site may have started as a website directory, but it quickly moved to add a keyword search engine, then a personalized news service, then a virtual community with bulletin boards and chat, then a free e-mail service, then a series of city guides for major U.S., European, and Asian destinations, then a travel guide, then a personal finance center, then a complete e-shopping guide sponsored by Visa. Then it acquired its way into the business of opening and hosting low-cost Web storefronts for budding merchants.

As it keeps forcing shifts in the market, Yahoo has managed to maintain the single largest daily audience of any website, attract the largest share of advertising and sponsorship revenue, while incidentally turning a respectable profit at a time when profitable e-commerce companies were scarce.

All this activity has mesmerized investors and has had the potential to confuse users of the service. They may never have high brand knowledge of all of Yahoo's many services, but Yahoo has succeeded in differentiating itself from the pack and boosting its brand esteem, its perceived popularity. Yes, the site has been in a constant state of flux since its launch. But cofounder Jerry Yang argues that customers have come to expect this. "We're a Web experience brand," Yang says. "And I think our customers understand that."

Yet Yahoo also seems to be scrambling, getting itself into the features game, without a clear message that it all adds up to some sort of meaningful solution to a specific set of problems. "We want to be the only place that anyone has to go to—to find and get connected to anything or anybody," says Yahoo CEO Timothy Koogle. That, in a nutshell, is what Yahoo is all about, he says. Can he be a little more vague?

Luckily, Yahoo's rivals in the Internet portal race seem to be scrambling even more frantically to develop the ultimate, overarching Web experience solution. That's the nature of business on the Web. Still, danger always lurks. At any point, some other brand could appear out of nowhere and shift the context of the digital landscape right out in front of all of us.

EXECUTIVE SURVIVAL GUIDE
SOLUTION BRANDING

▶ Identify a problem area facing either consumers or businesses, a set of issues that no one else is doing a good job of addressing.

▶ Use the interactive attributes of the Web to develop a comprehensive, multistep solution to that problem domain.

▶ Take into account that perhaps the Web itself cannot provide the total solution. You may have to tie your Web service together with a process that happens offline, in person, in a traditional business channel.

▶ Pay attention to all four pillars of building brand equity in the marketplace: differentiation, relevance, esteem, and knowledge.

▶ As you define what your solution brand stands for, make sure you can differentiate it from everything else on the market. And make sure it is relevant to the lives of your target customers.

▶ Don't rule out using mass media, such as television and print, to help build brand esteem, attaching emotional attributes to the brand. This type of emotional branding doesn't work well on the Web, which is why mass media and interactive media can reinforce one another.

▶ Don't just wait for the competitive environment, the brand context, to shift. By then it could be too late. Shift happens. Your job is to actively cause such shifts, constantly defining the evolution of the marketplace.

ALLOW YOUR PRICES TO FLUCTUATE FREELY WITH SUPPLY AND DEMAND

The Power of Dynamic Pricing

As a former fighter pilot for the British Royal Air Force, Marcus de Ferranti was accustomed to a little excitement in his life. Yet at age 35, Ferranti found himself laboring in obscurity for the British government, working as a member of the deputy prime minister's deregulation task force. It was then, in 1996, that he was struck by an unusual idea: Why not create something like a stock exchange for telecommunications capacity? He observed the obvious: As dozens of governments around the world started loosening their iron grip on state-run telephone monopolies, it would trigger vast changes in the going rates for international telephone calls and data transmission. Companies and consumers would want to benefit from falling prices as soon as possible.

Markets would turn chaotic. There was no doubt that both the usage and transmission capacity of phone and data lines would be surging at the same time that costs would be dropping. Prices for phone calls could be hugely different depending on where in the world the call was made and where the connecting phone company was located. "I began thinking: Companies would need to buy and sell network capacity from each other rapidly," Ferranti says. "We were bound to have a commoditized industry. And you need to trade any commodity on an appropriate, open market. The Internet is the best tool for enabling this trading."

How odd: Extra room on phone and data networks being traded like pork bellies and stock options? It was a provocative enough concept. But what could Ferranti do to pull it off? He teamed up with a colleague, a 37-year-old former banker named Richard Elliott, and the two set up shop in Ferranti's house in a leafy southwest London neighborhood. They put up a website called Band-X—short for bandwidth exchange—and invited thousands of telephone companies from around the world to post buy and sell orders on it.

This is how Band-X works: Say that a major international phone company saw that it would have some excess capacity between London and Frankfurt. In other words, an entire transmission switch would be going unused for several months—as wasteful as if expensive office space remained vacant. The switch, for instance, would be able to handle 90 simultaneous voice conversations at once. Perhaps another company with not enough capacity to serve its customers would pay to use it?

How much would a smaller, fast-growing telephone company that needs the resource pay for that? Perhaps the small company would offer $264,000 to lease it for a month. The big company would post basic information and its asking price on Band-X—and see whether there were any takers. Band-X accepts both buy orders (posted online in blue) and sell orders (posted in red) and matches them up with one another as best it can. All the while, the name of the companies posting these orders are kept anonymous, so as not to tip off their secret needs and desires to competitors. Such anonymity is exactly what makes stock and commodities markets function so well too.

"We decide whether [any given buyer and seller] are a suitable match," Ferranti says. "We check whether current regulations will allow it, whether commercially these two companies will get along, plus the technical aspects of whether these two companies can physically connect their networks together."

Entrenched forces scoffed at the plan. The dominant telecom companies, such as AT&T, and those with an even more recent history of government ownership, such as Deutsche Telekom, inherently dread the idea that their excess capacity could be a commodity subject to the brutal forces of supply and demand. They had been getting away with overcharging for quite a while. "The big established monopolies that have had control of a cartel for nearly 100 years don't like this at all," the Band-X cofounder says. "There used to be no correlation between costs and the prices that they could charge." Consumers, for instance, might end up paying $1.19 per minute for an international call that cost the phone company 6 cents per minute.

But many of the thousands of upstarts in this exploding industry jumped at the chance. "All these new entrants have had trouble getting realistic prices from those guys," the cofounder says. "Now we can having open pricing."

Nearly 4,000 representatives of telephone companies in 150 countries registered at the site in the first year, and Band-X successfully brokered more than 100 deals, worth a total of about $50 million. The company makes its money by taking an average 1 percent commission, which worked out to about $500,000 in first-year revenue.

To guide the players wondering what prices are indeed reasonable in this new market, Band-X publishes a live ticker tape that streams across the top page of its website. Like a stock ticker, the tape displays names of every country and a number reflecting the current, average cost per minute to make a telephone call into that country. When the ticker was established, each country began with an index set to 100. Since prices in this market usually drop or remain the same, but rarely go up, almost every country is now below that starting point. Denmark, for instance, was quoted at 72.4, whereas India's tightly controlled government phone system was still stuck on 100 for quite a while. Band-X's small staff is constantly researching going rates around the world to come up with the values.

But there was a major glitch with the business model. Far more deals that were initiated on the electronic exchange were falling through than were being completed. When Band-X made a match, it had to reveal the identities of the two companies to one another. Instead of a sale, it more often turned into the starting point for a protracted negotiation that could last up to six months. By then the price and the market could be completely different. "The price isn't fixed; it moves," Ferranti says. "This is the problem." Nearly 80 percent of the introductions Band-X made collapsed in negotiations.

Such matchups had to be done in real time. There was no other choice. So the two founders sprang for a switch of their own, buying a large network connection device from Northern Telecom. They keep it in Telehouse, which is one of the world's largest so-called point-of-presence (POP) locations. Telehouse is an immense structure bursting with wires and racks upon racks of phone network gear. Cables lead from the building, plunge underground, and sliver in the dark beneath the world's ocean floors to other POPs in far-off lands. For instance, there is a facility just like it on New York's Hudson Street. By owning its own switch, Band-X would be able to connect the telephone networks of buyers and sellers as soon as a match was made, before the players had the chance to haggle with one another.

This action enabled Band-X to boost the value of the deals it was completing to more than $60 million per month. It was the breakthrough that the company needed. The pricing of network bandwidth was happening on the fly, in close to real time, changing *dynamically* with the overall supply and demand in the marketplace. This was the initial idea behind the company, and Band-X was beginning to look like a success.

Once that happened, the typical problems and dilemmas of such start-ups set in. Naturally, the company started drawing competitors. One new foe, called Cape Saffron, started a similar service, but lifted a page from the online stock brokerage industry, charging a low, flat commission instead of a percentage of the transaction. Other new rivals were specializing only in telephone traffic that travels over the Internet itself, an essential new market that Band-X had to capture to remain competitive. The company was faced with the classic Darwinian situation: Grow fast and gain enough critical mass or die.

When venture capitalists caught word of the company, its success, and its situation, they started banging down the door. At a major European venture capital forum for high-tech investors, Ferranti along with dozens of other entrepreneurs made formal pitches to potential investors. At the conclusion of everyone's presentations, the typical scene erupted. "A lively squabble ensued among investors over which presenting company was most intriguing," reported an article in *Red Herring,* the Silicon Valley magazine that sponsored the forum. "For perhaps the first time, though, agreement was unanimous this summer: Every investor was captivated by London-based Band-X."

Some of the world's top venture-capital firms started offering Ferranti the typical deal that most Silicon Valley entrepreneurs salivate over and dream about: $3 million in seed money for 30 percent of the company's equity. Along with the money comes the halo effect: that some of the most savvy investors on the planet think you are hot stuff, a potential runaway success that could possibly bring a hundred-fold return on their investment.

Yet Band-X refused to take the money and run. It was actually turning a small profit on its own and "we thought we could get by without it," says the cofounder. "For the sake of few million dollars, the last thing we want is for the VC [venture capitalist] to be looking for the exit as fast as possible." What he means is that the high-tech venture capitalist always wants to sell the company or take it public within two or three years, make a return on his money, and use it to invest in the next series of deals. That's the upside potential. The downside risk is that it could take longer than that to turn any given start-up into a real, stable business, and pretty soon the VC gets itchy and starts dictating how to run the company or, in the worst case, forcing a premature sale or liquidation.

"We're better off sticking to our guns," Ferranti says. "Each day we delay taking money, we make it easier for us to survive organically."

Still, he says, it would be nice to raise just $500,000, in return for a much smaller equity stake, to buy an additional telecom switch or maybe even move to a real office. But venture capitalists these days consider that amount of money too small to bother with, he notes. The potential reward isn't big enough, so it's not worth their time and effort.

Some of the problems Band-X encountered weren't so typical but were very specific to the telecommunications industry. Some of the most sought-after matchups involve getting cheap bandwidth into the remaining nations with government monopolies. This can be accomplished by so-called leakies, gray-market companies that leak excess capacity into the marketplace at cut-rate prices. "It's like landing soldiers on the beach at night," he says. It can be done, but countries such as India are vigilant about policing leakies. Colombia sort of allows it, and its prices are down 7 percent because of it, but you sometimes have to deal with dangerous people. Meanwhile, in Nigeria, annoyed government officials have been known to arrest phone rebels and chop off their hands with a hatchet.

Despite these little hazards, market forces are on the side of

Band-X. As the walls come down, as more and more free-market bandwidth becomes available at the same time that more and more consumers demand less-expensive telephone and Internet service, dynamic pricing is likely to hold sway over the future of telecommunications.

Using the Web to Collect Demand

Dynamic pricing has not only descended like a tornado whipping through business-to-business markets such as telecommunications, but it is also spiraling to new levels of sophistication in consumer markets such as travel.

An airplane seat is as perishable as a tomato. If the airline doesn't sell seat 38C to Chicago by take-off, it's worthless and must be discarded like any piece of rotten fruit. Yet the average flight on a major carrier is at least 30 percent empty and 500,000 seats typically fly empty every day. Filling those seats without deflating the higher prices paid by other passengers is a tricky task. True, there is almost no incremental cost to flying a full plane, save for a few extra bags of peanuts or plastic trays of chicken. And the reward is great, as analysts have estimated that flying at full capacity doubles or triples profits. But no one who has paid $600 for a ticket wants to find out that the guy sitting next to him paid $60.

Jay S. Walker calls it the "markdown paradox," and he was pondering this problem when he stumbled onto an intriguing solution. A former world champion Monopoly tournament winner who grew up in Yonkers, New York, Walker in 1995 started a small intellectual property "laboratory" with the mission of using the Internet to recast age-old business methods. This particular problem cut across many industries: Companies that market their products and advertise their prices often need to sell excess inventory at greatly reduced prices. But if customers flocked to the lower prices, it could obliterate their normal retail price structure. As Walker puts it, "Does Ralph Lauren want to announce that his goods are available on the cheap at an outlet mall in New Jersey?"

The answer, Walker surmised, would be to take orders from customers over the Web. Those customers would simply name their own price for a product or service. The bid would be relayed to a seller or a series of sellers to see if anyone would bite. Walker's 25-employee company, Stamford, Connecticut–based Walker Digital, applied for a U.S. patent on this business method as well as some 250 other technology-related business models. Whether or not one believes that the very notion of obtaining a patent on the way you do business is patently absurd, it does not take away from the fact that Walker has something valuable on his hands.

In 1997 the 41-year-old Walker transferred this business concept to a new company, also based in Stamford, and called the new firm Priceline. In the spring of 1998 Priceline began offering airline tickets over the Web. Travelers log onto the site and start using it the same way they would any online reservation system, entering their destination, their departure and return dates, and the number of people in their party. But then Priceline asks for something unusual: how much the customer is willing to pay for each round-trip ticket. The dollar amount can be as low as the customer chooses. If you're flying from Boston to Toronto and only want to pay $100, the Priceline service will simply go ahead and try to find you a ticket for $100.

But this is not a shopping service, to be used to compare prices with other sources. "The way we're sure you want to go to Toronto is that you've given us your credit card number and authorized us to charge it if we find a ticket at that price," Walker says. In other words, the low price requires the buyer to take a risk and make a commitment. "We might not succeed," Walker says. "It's hard to get from Boston to Toronto at that price. I think there is only one direct connection."

That's why Priceline also asks how flexible the customer is. After asking you to name your price, it asks if you must fly direct, or if you are willing to change planes once, twice, or even three times. It also asks if you are willing to depart from and return to other nearby airports, in this case airports in Providence, Rhode Island, or Manchester, New Hampshire, that are more than an hour away from Boston.

Even after indicating how flexible you are, you may or may not get your desired ticket. "Uncertainty is injected into the process in order to serve both buyers and sellers," Walker says. "If we knew that we could get you the ticket for $100, then everyone would want one. If you need specificity, then you can't use this service. If you need to know you're flying in the morning, then don't use Priceline. The airlines can already do that for you. They wouldn't need us. Our system allows for determination of flexibility. Your flexibility will become a variable."

In its first seven months in business, Priceline sold 100,000 airline tickets this way, fulfilling most bids from travelers. The system worked because Walker signed up 20 airlines as partners. He won't say who they are because the airlines told him that they don't want this to disrupt their retail price structure. While it's been rumored that TWA and Southwest are both participants, neither Walker nor the airlines will confirm or deny that. "I don't know any sellers who *don't* want to protect their current distribution system."

In August of 1998 Walker received word from the U.S. Patent Office. His concept of "buyer-driven commerce" had received patent No. 5,794,207.

Priceline was the first system of its kind to win the participation of most major carriers because the airlines needed an independent clearinghouse to make this process work for them. American Airlines and several other carriers had already been unloading some cheap, weekend leisure fare trips at the last minute using the Web.

But the number of tickets sold this way had been so small that it has been inconsequential to the airlines' pricing structure. This seemed like a golden opportunity for the airlines to rid themselves of large numbers of unsold seats.

Like a travel agent, Priceline issues tickets from all carriers, so the customer never really knows if the ticket was obtained through traditional channels or through a secret partner arrangement. The goal is to maintain the willing participation of the sellers. "For a dynamic pricing system to work effectively, you need *both* sellers and buyers," he says, grappling for an apt analogy. "If there are no girls at the party, it's no fun."

Walker considers Priceline "a demand collection system." The primary competition to Priceline, he says, "is the car and the couch." Airlines have always known that there are a large number of people who would take more trips if flights were dramatically cheaper. But never before was there an efficient way of finding these customers.

Is this the ideal way to buy airline tickets? Walker admits that it is not for everyone, and he doesn't expect exacting business executives to use it much. Many travelers cannot be flexible most of the time. However, he thinks that there are millions of possible leisure trips that will be taken as a result of dynamic pricing that wouldn't have happened otherwise.

How does Priceline make money? It simply tries to buy the ticket from the airline for about $10 less than the customer offers. If it cannot buy the Toronto ticket for $90 within 24 hours, it will reject the customer's offer. While $10 may seem like peanuts, it is actually better than the $3 per ticket that American's massive Sabre reservation system collects in commissions. And in some years Sabre makes higher profits than all domestic airlines combined.

This dynamic pricing model works for other products and services as well. Indeed, Walker thinks it works even better for buying cars. "The airline industry has a very concentrated group of sellers who exert enormous power over pricing," he says. "In autos, with 25,000 dealers nationwide, we don't have to cater as much to the sellers."

When Priceline users are ready to buy a car, they send in the dollar amount they want to pay for a specific model and configuration, and the system tries to find a car from a nearby dealer at that price. Walker says there is one stipulation here that doesn't apply to airline tickets. The buyer must usually bid at least $1 higher than the dealer invoice price, so that the seller has a chance of making a profit. Typical bids are in the range of $300 over dealer invoice, he says. But the same commitment applies: When a buyer sends in her bid, she agrees to take possession of the car at the price she named.

This differs from other, better-known car buying services on the Web. For instance, Autobytel, Autoweb, and Microsoft's Carpoint will allow consumers to choose which car model they want to buy. Their personal purchase request is then sent over the Web to a local dealer who sends back a firm, no-haggle, low price. "Autobytel and Carpoint are *lead-generation* services," Walker notes. In other words, when a customer sends in his information and a dealer gets back to him with a price, the customer then decides whether to buy at that price or not.

"Lead generation services are silly," Walker insists. "They're the best of a bad set of choices. I really don't want to go on the Net and then have a car salesman call me." The whole point is to bypass the car salesman in the first place. "We tell customers that we found a dealer, go pick up your car. They can't sell you add-ons or rustproofing."

Priceline doesn't even provide the customers' names to the dealers until a deal is struck. "We don't waste anyone's time," Walker says. "Autobytel will give a dealer 100 leads and it may close six of them. We give them six deals and close them all." Priceline also differs from Autobytel in the way it generates revenue. Whereas Autobytel has recruited a network of 3,000 or so dealers who pay about $40,000 per year membership for sales leads in an exclusive territory, Priceline simply charges the consumer $25 and the dealer $75 after a successful transaction is completed. Dealers don't have to join the network in order to participate.

Under Priceline's vision of dynamic pricing, the price is being set by the consumer's own demand rather than the seller's guess at what the consumer is willing to pay. But even Walker acknowledges that variable pricing requires additional effort. "It's wonderful to walk into Wal-mart and get the same low price whether you are a sultan or a peasant. You don't want to haggle over items like toothpaste." Drawing on the Yiddish word for madness, Walker says, "That would be total *meshugas.*"

But for big-ticket transactions, dynamic pricing is often a better way to go. There is no such thing as a fixed price on a house, for instance. In addition to offering airline tickets and cars, Priceline has expanded into hotel reservations and home mortgages. Plus, it has designs on financial services, high-end retail, cellular phones, and business-to-business applications such as buying electricity, heating oil, and advertising space. He might even try to muscle into Band-X's business. If the practice spreads, the way we think about pricing will be obliterated. In this sense, Jay Walker's name is fitting, as he is certainly treading an unconventional, even forbidden, path.

Based on his early success, Walker has secured all the trappings of a company that has its eyes on the big time. He has raised a whopping $100 million in venture funding, launched an expensive mass advertising campaign, and stepped up hiring, to several hundred employees. At the same time, he's stepped back to become chairman of the board, while hiring a big-time CEO, Richard Braddock, a former president of Citicorp, to run day-to-day operations.

Overall, Walker's goal is to achieve nothing less than an evolutionary breakthrough in the world of business or, as he puts it, "to rewrite the DNA in dozens of industries." The Internet, he argues, has the power to challenge almost every assumption about business as we know it. "The great victory of our age is the victory of imagination over current belief," he says. "We, as a culture, have embraced the Star Trek ethos—that if you can imagine it and it has a technological base to it, it's probably going to happen."

Coming Full Circle

Dynamic pricing is the inevitable result when supply and demand are allowed to battle back and forth freely and ruthlessly. As practiced by Priceline, Band-X, and others, dynamic pricing creates a market in which the value of each piece of merchandise will fluctuate freely and continuously, and buyers and sellers will wield every tool available to them in their struggle to prevail over one another.

This is very different from walking into a store, or any marketplace, seeing a price tag, and deciding whether you want to buy at the posted price. We tend to take this notion of *fixed* retail pricing for granted, as if this were the only way to do things. But fixed pricing, as a practice, is fairly recent and very Western. In the United States, fixed pricing dates back only about 125 years, when mass retail pioneers such as Aaron Montgomery Ward and Frank W. Woolworth popularized the practice. Before that customers had to haggle for just about everything. And in the marketplaces and bazaars of Turkey, Indonesia, and India, things haven't changed much over time—if there is any posted price at all, it's usually just the starting point for a negotiation.

New forms of transportation and communication have always influenced the way goods are priced. Beginning in the mid-1800s, networks of railroads and canals permitted mass distribution of mass-produced items, making fixed pricing plausible for the first time. Meanwhile, the telegraph became a pervasive business-to-business medium among traders, bankers, investors, merchants, entrepreneurs, and captains of industry. Whereas prices for retail goods became fixed, products such as coal, wheat, and pork bellies became dynamically priced commodities because information about them, especially current prices, could be relayed quickly for the first time. All of these changes increased the number of buyers and sellers, creating and greatly expanding markets.

At the retail level, we've come full circle. Perhaps it's no coincidence that the original store to fix prices at 5 cents and 10 cents, the Woolworth's chain, has been completely liquidated, while Montgomery Ward has been closing dozens of stores during its protracted bankruptcy proceedings. Meanwhile, haggling, bidding, custom costing, and rapid-response pricing are emerging as mandatory Web economy survival strategies. Fixed mass merchandise pricing won't go away. It still makes sense for a wide variety of small-ticket items in a wide variety of settings. But dynamic pricing—in which an individual buyer and an individual seller come to an agreement for a specific deal at an instant in time—makes even more sense for many electronic transactions.

Once again communications technology is enabling the shift. On the Web, consumers are within reach of more market information than ever before, allowing them to compare goods and prices with a few mouse clicks. At the same time, producers have more information about each consumer and his or her needs. In this environment, price wars take on a different connotation. Instead of sellers slashing prices to win market share, we have buyers and sellers locked in an arms race in which each party is trying to use up-to-the-minute data to gain the upper hand.

It's not totally unfamiliar territory. Street merchants in big cities will typically charge $5 for an umbrella—unless it starts raining, whereby the price instantly jumps to $15. Conversely, there's the Sy Syms model. Based in the Northeast, the Syms clothing chain, "where an educated consumer is our best customer," pioneered the notion of prices for an individual garment dropping every two weeks if no one buys it. A suit priced at $850 can plunge to $575 and then to $365 and then to $188 and then to $79.95 if there are no takers. Finally, you—yes you—are suddenly the proud owner of the world's ugliest and formerly most overpriced suit.

Forms of network-enabled pricing have dominated the airline industry for years. Airfares for each trip are dependent on exactly when you book and how many seats are left on the flight. Consumers initially hated the so-called yield management model, since it is in place solely to maximize revenue for the airlines, but they have come to accept it and expect it. Just as they have come to expect that certain products will be on special sale after Christmas. Or just as a wily ticket scalper hikes his premium when a show sells out or drops it when the event begins.

In the Web economy, it's possible to drop or raise your prices depending not only on when someone is buying but also based on who is buying, how often they shop, and in response to overall supply, demand, and competition.

Economists note that uniform prices actually cost sellers revenue. Some customers would have paid more than the posted price for, say, an Oriental rug or a refrigerator. Others, instead of balking, would have paid less but still enough to leave the seller with a net profit. The problem with the alternative, putting all retail goods up for bidding and haggling, is that the process is incredibly time consuming and labor intensive. In traditional retail, there aren't enough people to manage it. Those who set the list prices are not there at the point of sale. In the mass consumer society of the twentieth century, uniform pricing made the most sense.

But on the Web, software can take care of all that work, offloading the haggling so that people don't have to do it. Only with the advent of the Web can transaction costs be lowered sufficiently to bring the bidding model of retail back into vogue for a huge base of customers. These are the reasons why dynamic, everchanging, customized pricing should work particularly well in the fragmented information society of the twenty-first century.

Dynamic pricing is a sophisticated survival strategy that can balance lopsided power arrangements. Whereas many producers have feared that hypercompetition would reduce all prices and products to commodity levels, thus tilting the balance too far in favor of consumers, this competitive bidding model strikes what could be an ideal equilibrium, in which the forces of supply and demand are played out in vigorous bidding contests.

Whether dynamic pricing will work for your business depends on a number of factors. Will your customers object to these new pricing models? Will they become infuriated at constantly changing costs? Will this throw a serious monkey wrench in your ability to predict your revenue and profits? Will savvy online shoppers figure out how to outsmart the software and the built-in pricing mechanisms at major e-commerce hubs? Will it maximize revenue? Could it cannibalize your existing price structure? Even if you answered "maybe" to all these questions, dynamic pricing may still be the right way to go. For if your competitors succeed with it first, it may be too late.

Taking Advantage of Digital Bazaars

Online auction houses are already bringing dynamic pricing to the masses. These wild and woolly digital bazaars represent one of the fastest-growing segments of electronic commerce. By 1998 more than 200 online auction sites sold more than $1 billion worth of computers, consumer electronics, antiques, collectibles, used cars, and just about anything else that one person may want, but another may want even more. Often the competitive gaming aspect of these contests makes the experience entertaining, much more so than your average online shopping excursion.

At auction sites, consumers decide what an item is worth to them. The seller simply sets a suggested opening price, then buyers bid on what they want, offering higher and higher bids until a preset expiration time, when the highest bidder wins.

Most of the products auctioned off by the top Web bidding sites have something rather subtle in common: No one really can say precisely what they are worth. A brand-new, current-model personal computer has a keenly understood and extremely narrow price range, as sale prices are constantly published in magazines, newspaper ads, and all over the Web. But what should a phased-out 266 megahertz Pentium PC go for? How about a slightly outmoded stereo system? Or a refurbished Macintosh? Or last year's model of golf clubs? Or a basketball autographed by Michael Jordan? Or a Caribbean cruise departing next Wednesday? No one can really say.

For many people, these items are worth next to nothing. But for some people, these items are very valuable. In any case, there is usually no reliable price list to go by. Auctions thrive on such ambiguity. "The value is not predetermined, so the buyer has a responsibility to understand the value of the object to *them*," says Jerry Kaplan, the CEO of Onsale Inc., a top auction site. "You simply need a willing buyer and a willing seller at a given price. That's the whole point of having an auction."

To understand the value of the process to all parties involved, we have to witness a simple transaction. One typical auction at Onsale.com began on a Thursday morning, with initial bidding starting at $199 for a lot of 93 factory-refurbished, Hewlett-Packard OfficeJet 520s, which are all-in-one color printing, faxing, copying, and scanning machines. At the time, both Staples and CompUSA had the same machine quoted for $350 in their catalogs.

Is there a catch? Sort of. At the same time the auction was going on, H-P was planning to announce a new, more advanced line of OfficeJets, the 700 series. Only people in the industry or very sophisticated consumers would know this. (The only way I knew it was that H-P coincidentally mailed me an advance press release the day the auction began.)

Naturally, H-P was quietly planning to slash the suggested retail prices for the models that were up for auction—down to $300 and possibly heading lower—then discontinue them altogether. Some traditional retailers were just getting around to lowering their prices in anticipation. So we had a situation here in which the perceived value of these printers for many bidders was temporarily higher than the market value. I decided to use the information to influence the bidding. Since all active bids are listed for public view, I posted a short message—HP TO ANNOUNCE 700/SLASH 520 PRICES—in the comment line next to my initial $209 bid.

The notice came too late for some. A few bidders had already offered between $279 and $299. They clearly weren't getting much of a good deal at all, given the $20 shipping cost and the fact that these machines may have been in prior use as demo models or some such. Meanwhile, my bid for $209 was initially among those in line to win one of the machines. But by the following Monday morning, just before the high noon bidding deadline, there were more than 100 bids that were higher. So I upped my price to $229, which turned out to be the minimum bid required to win.

Most of the bidders did pretty well. HP did well because it unloaded these machines at an opportune time. And Onsale, thanks to a few overzealous bidders, very likely made a narrow profit on the allotment. Kaplan says that winners typically buy for 15 to 20 percent below comparable retail prices for brand-new machines. The fact that buyers usually don't make out like bandits is absolutely necessary for the system to work. In the world of dynamic pricing, the deck is very rarely stacked in favor of either the buyer or the seller. Brutal market forces ensure that. As they say in Negotiation 101, both parties have to feel as if they have won something.

Overall, the auction model has been a success for Onsale. The number of registered bidders broke the 1 million mark after barely two years in business. According to Kaplan, about half of those bidders buy for personal use and about half buy on behalf of their companies for business use. By its fourth year online, Onsale had a mixed record of profitability but had surpassed $200 million in revenue. Most important, notes Keith Benjamin, a research analyst with Robertson Stephens, "it has validated the online auction format for suppliers in need of a reliable channel for quickly selling close-out products."

The lesson here is *not* that you should want to start a new online auction house. Rather, it's a lesson about pricing that applies to countless companies across dozens of industries. If your business sells a product or a service that either rapidly depreciates in value over time, like a computer, or perishes at a certain instant, like an airline ticket, then you must consider online auctions as a key new sales channel.

Caveat Emptor

The curious thing about online auctions is how a select few of them have gone on to become such huge success stories, while countless others struggle to exist in the shadows and teeter on the edge of going out of business. In this sense, online auctions are a classic evolutionary game of chicken-and-egg. If there aren't enough buyers, competition and prices are depressed, which keeps sellers away. And if there aren't enough sellers, the auction won't attract buyers.

The two most well-known auctions, Onsale Inc. and eBay Inc., have managed to attract so many buyers and sellers that they are already teeming with life. Thriving in such an environment is often a matter of being first to offer a unique format or a targeted set of products, being reliable, and providing easy-to-use bidding software. But another factor is being able to fight the pernicious forces of fraud.

"Our industry is full of defaulters," says Ferranti of Band-X. "There's an enormous community of people who will stiff you. They change their company name and disappear into the blue yonder, and this happens not just in the countries that you might expect but in the U.S. in particular." To combat fraud and errant behavior, such as failing to pay for services rendered or not responding to valid offers, Band-X will revoke a defaulter's membership in the exchange and publish his or her name and company on a public blacklist.

At eBay, the leading "person-to-person" auction site, fraud can be "a pretty big problem," says eBay founder Pierre Omidyar, a Silicon Valley entrepreneur who started the service as a hobby, in part so that his girlfriend could buy and sell Pez dispensers with fellow collectors. Nowadays, as a profitable, public corporation, eBay, as well as many of its more than 1 million registered members, has to work extra hard at exposing the few scam artists among them. "People complain about it online and we are always receiving tip-offs," Omidyar says. "It raises the ire of our community."

In the world of Web auctions, there are several ways of staging a swindle. Failing to deliver an item to a buyer who has already sent you a check in advance is only the most obvious ripoff. Others are more subtle because they exploit the fact that online bidders are all in separate locations. In a traditional face-to-face auction, the auctioneer can place a shill in the audience. The practice is unethical as well as illegal in some states, but at least buyers have visual clues. If a lady in a red hat keeps making bids that seem designed only to drive up the final price, buyers can back off. On the Web, since you can't see the lady or the red hat, you have no way of knowing.

While the vast majority of transactions are completed safely, online auctions have become the number-one scam on the Internet, according to statistics compiled by the Internet Fraud Watch unit of the National Consumers League (NCL), a century-old protection group in Washington, D.C. Overall reports of Internet fraud increased sixfold in 1998 as compared to the previous year, the group says. Since they are so new, Web auctions didn't even merit a separate fraud category in 1996, says Susan Grant, an NCL vice-president. But they suddenly became responsible for 68 percent of the several thousand total Internet-related fraud complaints the group received. She calls that figure "the tip of the iceberg" because most consumers do not bother to report such incidents.

Some consumers who filed complaints claim to have detected shills after the fact, by tracing a disproportionate number of last-minute bids back to a single Internet server computer, Grant says.

And of course, consumers can't actually see the goods up for Web auction. If you are buying a rug that is described in the on-line description as hand-made in Persia, it could very well be machine-made in Taiwan. "It's hard enough to tell [whether something is authentic] when you're looking right at it," adds Grant. "It's virtually impossible on the Web."

At eBay, anyone who bids or sells something must register his or her name, address, and e-mail address. (If your e-mail address is with Hotmail, Excitemail, or another free service, the system will likely reject you, because those services do not require credit cards and therefore people can make up an identity while registering.) Once successfully registered, members can list their items and make use of the site's bid management software for a fee, usually ranging from 25 cents to $2, depending on how prominently the item is displayed. If the item sells, eBay charges the seller a commission ranging up to 5 percent.

Since so many items are being sold at a given time, the auction manager can't possibly police every deal. Even so, the company claims that fraud is rare. According to San Jose–based eBay Inc., only 27 auctions of the roughly 1 million occurring in a recent four-month period involved possible criminal action. Records of the potentially fraudulent transactions are forwarded to the U.S. Postal Service and law enforcement groups, the company says.

The primary way members fight fraud is via an extensive feedback system in which members rate the reputations of everyone who does business there. In an attempt to mimic face-to-face trust, members submit comments about the sellers from which they buy. A positive comment earns the seller a point, while a point is deducted for each negative posting. Some online sellers with stellar reputations have ratings of 50 or 100 or even 1,000. The points have become so valuable that they have been known to become the subject of disputes in divorces. One can imagine the settlement: You can keep the car, jerk, as long as I get the eBay points.

"If you're bidding on an item, we encourage you to look up the reputation of the seller first," Omidyar says. The company cancels the accounts of traders with excessively negative reputations, mostly obtained by failing to deliver merchandise, misrepresenting the quality of their goods, or being suspected of submitting shill bids. Omidyar says that he typically must kick 20 to 50 people per month off the service. The feedback system thus works as an organic immune system, attempting to isolate dangerous intruders and eradicate them before they can do harm. All online auctions, however, are a buyer-beware world. Along with the price benefits come certain risks.

Watch Out for Shopbots

Pricing strategies become even more complex when your online business is besieged by shopbots, the new species of pesky programs that traverse the Web, searching for the best deal on behalf of their master, perhaps even engaging in a negotiation for something and actually purchasing it.

A very simple shopbot is available for participants of the Onsale auction. Called BidMaker, this program enables buyers to participate in an auction without having to monitor price fluctuations. For instance, let's say that a cruise for two of the Greek Islands that departs in two weeks is being auctioned off at a starting price of $99. News of deals like this typically draws interest from hundreds or thousands of spontaneous vacation goers around the world. So chances are this cruise will go for much higher than $99. You can instruct BidMaker that you are only willing to pay as much as $499. This way the software will engage in rounds of bidding for you, then inform you via e-mail whether you've won or are about to lose. Either way, you do not have to be present at the site for days as the contest proceeds.

The promise of software bots that hunt the infosphere on behalf of users has been a constant refrain for years. And judging by the sheer number and the frantic activity of these supposedly smart splices of code, it's clear that shopbots themselves are developing in a Darwinian fashion, battling each other and market forces for supremacy and even giving birth to smarter and smarter offspring—in the form of new releases and versions of themselves.

Capable of working on their own, the most useful shopbots labor in background mode, searching through files and trading messages with other people's bots. Think of them as digital valets that toil away while master or madam concentrates on more important tasks on—or away from—the computer.

Shopbots are the most recent progeny of so-called intelligent agents, a type of software first envisioned in the 1960s by Oliver Selfridge, then a computer scientist at the Massachusetts Institute of Technology's Lincoln Laboratory. Now living in Cambridge, Selfridge says that a true intelligent agent does not merely automate certain tasks but actually learns as it goes along and makes decisions on its own. Very few programs now on the market exhibit true intelligence in this sense, he says. When searching through databases and newswires, Selfridge continues, a truly intelligent agent would be able to teach itself how to do it faster, better, and more cheaply over time. Most of today's bots don't learn that way, he says, though "our children will see it."

Nowadays, almost every Web search engine and shopping site features its own shopbot. For instance, the Junglee bot, which searches for products available from hundreds of online merchants, was acquired by Amazon.com for a whopping $180 million in stock. Yahoo, Hotbot, and Snap are among the sites that offer their own branded version of the program. Meanwhile, Infoseek acquired a bot called Quando that it deploys. And Excite features the Jango shopbot, which it snapped up in 1997.

The initial versions of these shopbots exhibit very little ability to learn over time, either about the changing conditions of the market or about the preferences of the users who launch the searches. They merely scan websites and spit back a list of products sorted by make, model, or price. If you enter in "digital phone," these programs may just offer a list of dozens or hundreds of such phones. If you narrow the price range to under $100, the list will shrink. If you enter the brand name and model number, they will provide links to sites that offer the cheapest prices on exactly what you want. They're certainly helpful, but they are not the agents that Selfridge had envisioned.

As shopbots get smarter, their behavior may get more and more unpredictable, even downright dangerous to the health of online markets.

That is one striking discovery stemming from a series of shopbot simulations conducted at IBM's Institute for Advanced Commerce in Hawthorne, New York. Once shopbots really proliferate and become better at finding what people want at the best possible price, the IBM researchers say, they could trigger mindless price wars that ultimately hurt both sellers and buyers— in a way that resembles Wall Street's automated trading programs.

"There's potential for a lot of mayhem once bots are introduced on a wide scale," says Jeffrey Kephart, manager of the IBM group studying bots, intelligent software agents, and other so-called emergent phenomena. The goal, he says, is to find ways to avert such chaotic scenarios, especially as the Web turns into "a seething milieu" populated with billions of bots.

In their simulation of a futuristic shopbot economy, the IBM researchers set up in-baskets for 10,000 buyers of news articles. About 500 shopbot programs mediated between the bots working on behalf of consumers and the bots representing about a dozen publishers, or sellers. The shopbots were instructed to purchase articles from a publisher and sell them to as many consumers as it could. The result: Periods of relative calm in the market and brief prosperity for the publisher were punctuated by violent, sporadic price wars. "A never-ending cycle of fairly regular price wars ensues," the researchers wrote.

In the simplest price wars, two or more shopbots offering the same product (a set of news categories) keep undercutting one another until some or all of the sellers bail out of the general market and retreat to less competitive niche categories, leaving most customers entirely unserved.

Kephart is most interested in what happens when the Web economy is populated by billions of conflicting shopbots. If online sellers of everything from airline tickets and hotel rooms, to books and CDs, to cars and computers, to insurance and mortgages, want to remain in business, they will have to learn when to negotiate with shopbots and when to hold firm on prices. In addition, he says, shopbots will have to become much better at comparing qualitative aspects of different products, not just numerical prices.

Shopbots, however, will never be as intuitive as humans. "Automated agents are not people," Kephart's team notes. "They make decisions and act on them at a vastly greater speed. But they are immeasurably less sophisticated, less flexible, less able to learn, and notoriously lacking in common sense. Given these differences, it is entirely possible that bot-based economies will behave in very strange and unfamiliar ways."

Overall, no matter whether it's automated shopbots or real live people who are bidding on your products and services, it's vital to remember that you can control your own destiny to a large extent. Yes, the Web shifts massive power into the hands of buyers. But in the world of dynamic pricing, neither the buyer nor the seller should dominate. For the overall system to work, both sides in the negotiation must be part of an overall equilibrium. Buyers get a valuable product at a great price, while sellers boost revenue and profits by unloading certain types of goods and services at an opportune moment. At its core, dynamic pricing is all about timing.

EXECUTIVE SURVIVAL GUIDE:
DYNAMIC PRICING

▶ Recognize when certain of your products and services are nearing the end of the most productive part of their life cycle. Just as computers, software, airline tickets, or the unbooked time of a consultant can suddenly drop in value or become worthless, some of your offerings also may fall into the category of "excess inventory."

▶ Also recognize when certain deadlines or surges in demand can propel your prices upward. Just as certain toys are most valuable right before Christmas and event tickets can fetch enormous premiums, some of your offerings may suddenly become hot stuff.

▸ Sell your excess inventory and suddenly hot products through a dynamic pricing channel. Develop a special Web site or area of your site to unload products quickly, with the prices constantly changing to reflect supply and demand.

▸ To protect your normal pricing structure and to guard against the so-called markdown paradox, sell your goods on consignment to an online auction house, which in turn will sell to the end customer without giving the perception that you are undercutting or disturbing your regular prices.

▸ Take steps to guard against fraud that could become rampant in an online auction or dynamic pricing marketplace. Register all players, get credit card numbers, and post the names of fraudulent buyers or sellers for others to see.

▸ Make the proliferation of shopbots work to your advantage. Your site should be able to provide price and product information to these automated shopping programs and negotiate with them on your own terms.

LET AFFILIATE PARTNERS DO YOUR MARKETING FOR YOU

Befriending Potential Enemies

The germ of this contagious idea came from an unlikely source. Once upon a time, a woman passionate about the subject of divorce was running her own website. Naturally, the site was stocked with information and resources for helping wives who were struggling with the legal and emotional issues surrounding the dumping of their husbands. In the early part of 1996, this woman sent an e-mail message to suggestions@amazon.com. She mentioned that she already had a section on her site recommending useful books relating to divorce. Could she link her visitors to Amazon.com to purchase them? And by the way, if she did, shouldn't she earn a commission on those sales?

The suggestion took root, and the Amazon.com Associates Program was born that summer. Commissions would range from 5 to 15 percent depending on the type of the book and how much it was already discounted. "It was open to everyone, and it was free, and that's the beauty of it," says Shawn Haynes, who took over running the program that December, when there were already 4,000 affiliated sites.

According to Haynes, the original goals of the program were threefold: acquire new, loyal customers through these referrals, enable others to participate in online bookselling without having to fulfill book orders themselves, and "extend Amazon's editorial expertise into unique areas or spheres of influence" that, according to Haynes, would be impossible for the company to develop on its own—subjects ranging from finance, to kayaking, to fly fishing.

By the following summer, the number of affiliates had more than doubled, to 10,000, and the program became so successful at generating quick revenue growth that it spawned competition. Book giant Barnes & Noble launched its own affiliate network as part of its new Web commerce venture. It differed from Amazon's in two ways. Affiliates had to sign an exclusivity clause, meaning they couldn't be part of Amazon's program too. And partners would earn commissions on *all* books that referred customers bought during their online shopping session, not just the specific ones that were recommended on the affiliate's site. With its clout in the book business, B&N signed up some high-profile partners, including the high-impact site run by the *New York Times Book Review.* Amazon was soon forced to match the blanket commission deal.

Turns out, there was room in the growing online book market for both networks, and the competition didn't slow down Amazon's growth. By the beginning of 1998, Amazon had signed up a total of 30,000 affiliates. Then, after Amazon started selling a full range of music CDs as well, the number more than tripled, to a remarkable 100,000 affiliates by the summer. At that point, the associates program had clearly taken on the status of a viral epidemic, as the Amazon logo seemed as if it were everywhere. "We're expanding our presence to the far corners of the Web," Haynes declared. The program was clearly a major factor in accelerating revenue growth. Clearly, that long-forgotten divorced woman should have received more than a commission on selling a few books. But such is the nature of new ideas floating about the Web.

For Amazon, the associates program indeed had the intended effect of preempting other small players from directly competing with it. If anyone could earn $2 or $3 in pure profit selling a book or CD that another company was sourcing, shipping, and servicing, why in the world would you go directly into the book or music selling business yourself? The profit margins on these items aren't much better than that. Sure, Amazon has had to worry about the big guys, B&N and Borders. But it's out-and-out flattering to go up against such prestigious giants (especially as Amazon's stock market value grew to be greater than that of those two companies combined).

As a result, Amazon has harnessed the energy of countless potential enemies. Think of it this way: When you're in a jungle equipped with nothing but sharp senses and a trusty gun, it's far easier to fend off a couple of big targets than it is to avoid getting eaten alive by thousands of deadly insects. Through its associates program, Amazon has essentially befriended all of these potential online niche-market booksellers.

Click-Through Chaos

No company can afford to stand as an island in the Web economy. The electronic commerce ventures that are surviving and thriving are the ones that have formed an intricate relationship web, cooperating and sharing revenue and customer traffic with many partners at once. Affiliate networks are just the most popular way to bring the age-old practice of word-of-mouth advertising into a new *word-of-mouse* era.

There is no perfectly apt analogy for affiliate networks among traditional business models. It's like a pyramid scheme without the pyramid. Or maybe it's more like multilevel marketing without the multilevels. Or perhaps it's akin to franchising without actually offering exclusive franchises. Essentially, affiliate networks are the Web's unique way of roping others into doing your marketing for you.

Which is why they have such irresistible allure. For those who run them, there are no initial costs, save for any phone calls and employee hours required to recruit and manage a base of affiliates. Those expenses are small potatoes compared to the cost of placing advertising banners at potentially thousands of sites. And for the thousands of online partners who sign up, there seems to be nothing to lose. Since there are usually no joining fees, the only cost is the effort it takes to keep updating the banners and information on their own sites. Any commissions earned are gravy.

The fact that this sounds too good to be true—at least to neophytes—has led to a huge avalanche of such networks. Competition to sign up affiliates—from lone college students to well-known corporations—is growing exponentially more intense. And earning commissions is no longer as easy as programming in a few hyperlinks, heading out for long lunches, and waiting for checks to arrive in the mail. In fact, most affiliate programs are failing and most affiliated sites earn few or no commissions.

What is it that separates thriving programs from dying ones? Will this blend of direct marketing, franchising, and cooperative advertising quickly spread to every industry? Or will many of these programs end up behaving like traditional pyramid schemes, becoming less and less effective as more and more people try and do it?

What are some of the reasons that affiliate networks fail? Does it make sense eventually to put a limit on the number of members, just as traditional franchises do? In more traditional businesses, a manufacturing company, a restaurant chain, or service provider will recruit affiliates, offering them a lucrative franchise in return for exclusive rights to a specific sales territory. On the Web, however, such exclusivity is not as straightforward. "If you tried to locate a new Saturn dealer a half mile away from an existing one, they'd both freak," says James Marciano, CEO of Refer-it.com, a New York–based site that maintains a descriptive list of hundreds of affiliate networks. "You can't easily stake out territories on the Web."

What will happen as all this activity leads to a free-for-all atmosphere, in which greater numbers of websites that sell stuff are recruiting even greater numbers of affiliates? If a famous online bookseller, for instance, grants an unlimited number of affiliate agreements to websites that sell sports books, will any of them make a significant amount of money? Given the generous commission rates, is it even possible to make a profit on these referred transactions? Does it make better sense to charge a small fee for an online franchise license, then pay out larger commissions and build up a smaller but stronger network?

Reigning in the click-through chaos that exists in the marketplace begins with a question: How does the affiliate network fit into one's overall business? Amazon's Haynes won't say what percentage of sales come through affiliate referrals, except to point out that it's "a significant minority of our revenue." Independent estimates peg that share at anywhere between 5 and 15 percent of revenue. If you use an average commission rate of 10 percent, and you look at the approximately $600 million in sales Amazon posted in 1998, that works out anywhere between $30 million and $90 million paid out in commissions to its affiliates.

Some big affiliates, such as AOL.com, can earn millions of dollars in commissions, while others earn next to nothing. Since its top partners bring in a disproportionate amount of sales, Haynes has been working extra hard to sign custom deals with those kinds of big players.

For instance, Amazon signed a long-term, multimillion-dollar agreement with personal finance leader Intuit Inc., becoming the exclusive bookseller on Intuit's Quicken.com site in the United States and the preferred seller in the United Kingdom and Germany. Amazon receives extensive placements on Quicken.com sites and in its software, while Intuit earns rich commissions on every transaction.

Haynes doesn't rule out big changes for the associates program in the future. He says it all depends how the program serves Amazon's larger aims. What happens when Amazon switches gears and makes *profitability* it's number-one goal, instead of early-stage revenue growth and customer acquisition? It's no secret that Amazon makes little to no profit on sales that involve commission payments. What if the business context shifts? "If it no longer made sense," offers Haynes, "we would look at changes."

At first, affiliate programs seemed cool, so everyone gladly linked away without thinking twice. But think again: Some of these companies spend millions on marketing, with the aim of landing new customers. If an online retailer has to spend $30 to $200 on mass media advertising to land each new customer, and that same retailer is only paying $2 to an affiliated site for each paying buyer, who is getting the better of the deal? The retailer has a good chance at keeping that new customer as a loyal, revenue-generating asset for many years. Meanwhile, the affiliate diverted the attention of its own visitor and perhaps squandered it for good.

For affiliates, therefore, the program is not "free" at all. It is paying away the attention of their visitors, directing them to something else, someplace else. If you take your Web venture seriously, then you must carefully consider where that attention goes and whether it fits in with your overall mission.

As the Web evolves, a higher and higher percentage of people who click through from an affiliate to a major retail site will *already* be current customers. The value of that referral then becomes much lower from the retailer's point of view. What if these marketers decide to cut their commission rates or put more restrictions on them? How would that change the level of trust between that site and its thousands of partners? The answer is that trust would quickly turn to suspicion.

And that brings us to a larger point: You should always know what motivates your affiliate partners and watch whether changes in the environment also change their needs and goals. And affiliate partners likewise must understand what motivates the site to which they are referring their customers. It's a complicated dance of symbiotic relationships that can be suddenly disrupted by a merger, acquisition, or new competition. Anticipate how relationships can change and develop a plan to take advantage of that change first.

Traps and Pitfalls

The revenue-sharing concept has already spread to every product and service category under the sun, from artwork to Zambonis. But many of these smaller affiliates networks have been stuck in a rather primitive stage of evolution.

"We see it as the future," says Phillip Rose, managing director of the Lobster Net, a site that express-mails live and kicking lobsters packed in Styrofoam, wet newspapers, and seaweed to homes and businesses all over the United States. Rose has attracted hundreds of other websites into his own affiliates program. In return for including an ad banner that links to Lobster Net, these affiliates earn 5 percent commissions for every referred customer who actually orders a conscious crustacean.

Rose anticipates that his affiliated sites will drive the majority of sales in the future. After about a year or so in business, such referrals had accounted for about 10 percent of his 40 or so daily shipments. But Rose does more than run a lobster company. Rather, the entity that he and a partner run is called ProActive Marketing Inc. It sells not only lobsters over the Web but also jewelry, cigars, electronics, camping equipment, auto products, and—the perfect Web product—Dutch tulip bulbs. All have their own dedicated websites with their own legions of affiliates. Combined annual sales at the three-employee company has been about $1 million.

Rose is looking to his partners to drive sales to new heights. "To survive on the Internet, we have to make our affiliates as productive as possible," he says. "It's a numbers game, and 1,000 is better than one."

But if Rose really expects these partners to become such an integral part of his business, why is he only paying 5 percent? The competitive nature of the game has escalated to the point where that is not nearly enough. When a site called eToys.com launched its affiliate program, it initially began paying 12 percent of sales referred by its affiliates. "We realized we were shooting ourselves in the foot by being cheap," says Phil Polishook, eToys' vice president of marketing. When it doubled the rate to 25 percent, it began attracting more serious affiliates that would position its banner links more prominently and put its toys in a richer editorial context.

Besides offering incentives that are too low, Rose allows his affiliate programs to run themselves on virtual autopilot. The program is managed by ClickTrade, a company that provides software to automatically track the referrals and pay out the commissions. The software makes running an affiliate network deceptively simple. While Amazon.com has developed its own proprietary software to track click-throughs, credit the accounts with commissions, and mail out quarterly checks, most other programs, including rival BarnesandNoble.com, use less-expensive, off-the-shelf software such as ClickTrade and BeFree that automatically performs these chores.

These packages perform well for certain functions. But too many affiliate networks also rely on these companies to attract new affiliates into their program. Like Rose at ProActive Marketing, they may end up obtaining hundreds of new affiliates but few high-quality ones. Alas, ProActive has been a bit too passive in this regard. A disproportionate number of websites that join these programs fail to put any of these products in context. Many call themselves cybermalls and just maintain a series of banners so that users can click through and shop at various sites. Because they have no original content or unique services, these sites are cheap to set up. But they provide little value and end up with dismally low sales.

Instead, marketers should aim to attract partners that integrate their products into a meaningful whole. Clearly, the single best site for lobster referrals would be L.L. Bean, the Freeport, Maine–based catalog company that has made a major push into Web commerce. Customers are already ordering clothing and sporting gear fashioned in L.L. Bean's rugged, outdoor, seacoast image. Perhaps shopping at the site has put them in the mood for a lobster dinner. Landing L.L. Bean as an affiliate would be quite a catch indeed.

Another small business that is relying heavily on affiliates is Gallagher & Forsythe, a 25-year-old, family-owned wholesaler that operates the Shades.com and Swiss Army Depot sites. Based on Cape Cod, the company has annual sales of about $2 million, about one-third of which is attributable to its more than 2,500 online partners, says president Peter W. Adler.

Since announcing affiliate programs for the two sites, the company has been signing up 10 new partners per day. Affiliates earn 8 percent commissions on all referred customers who purchase sunglasses and 10 percent commissions on those who purchase pocket knives and other officially licensed Swiss Army brand products.

Like most entrepreneurs who run affiliate programs, a disproportionate percentage of Gallagher & Forsythe's sales comes from a small number of partners. In his case, Adler receives more than half of his customer referrals from a few big fish sites run by America Online, GTE, PC World, and Ameritech.

There's no doubt that these affiliate networks have given both sites a big boost. But Adler advises not to underestimate what it takes to sell merchandise on the Web. Awhile back, AT&T ran TV ads depicting two women who came up with an idea to sell unbreakable, rubber sunglasses online after getting shut out by major retail chains. By the end of the 30-second spot, the fictional duo had already set up the Web venture and then went off to sun themselves on a boat. "The AT&T ad was very clever," Adler says. "But it's a lot harder to be successful in sunglasses online than the ad made it appear. It takes a phenomenal effort. The commercial did lead to a huge surge in orders for our rubber sunglasses, though."

Displacing Advertising

With so many Web merchants running affiliate networks, you might think that all these sales referrals would add up to a quite a big chunk of change. And you'd be right. Jupiter Communications, a New York–based research firm, estimates that affiliate sales accounted for an impressive 11 percent of $5.7 billion of total on-line consumer transactions in 1998. What's more, Jupiter projects that percentage to grow to 24 percent of the $37.5 billion in on-line purchasing by consumers in 2002.

These numbers do not include business-to-business purchasing, but they do include special revenue-sharing deals between portals such as Yahoo and AOL.com and Web commerce sites such as Amazon.com and CDnow. Those bigtime relationships usually work on a commission basis as well but often involve even higher commission rates.

If you begin to think of a Web economy in which about $1 out of $4 of consumer spending is driven by these kinds of revenue-sharing programs, you begin to get a clue as to why the Web works so much differently from both traditional retail or traditional media. When, say, a department store places an ad in a newspaper or runs a TV commercial, it can never really know exactly how much sales those ads generated. Such ads are placed to build general awareness of the store or of a specific product promotion. But Web merchants that enable affiliates to place banners and product information on thousands of sites across the Web know precisely which sites drove exactly how much in sales. They have to tabulate that information in order to tally the quarterly commission payments.

The net effect is that affiliate networks actually are displacing advertising as we have come to know it in the Web economy. If those Jupiter projections are correct, affiliate sales are well on their way toward becoming a bigger business than online banner advertising, in which top media sites and search engines charge upfront for available space. Whereas sites from traditional media companies such as CNN, Time Warner, the *New York Times,* and *USA Today* continue to talk about selling their "inventory" of online ad space, affiliate networks are a powerful example of why charging for "space" in a digital environment where space is infinite makes little sense. Instead, more and more "ads" become like salesmen working purely on commission rather than something you pay for ahead of time regardless of the result it produces.

Just compare the return on investment: The average CPM (the cost per thousand metric that advertisers use to price advertising based on measured audience size) for placing a banner advertisement on a popular website has been about $30. If a typical 1 percent of people who see it click through to the marketer's site, and then 10 percent of *those* people actually go so far as to purchase something, you have only acquired 1 customer out of each 1,000. And it ends up costing you $30 to acquire that customer. But at $2 a pop or even $10 a pop, a paid affiliate referral is cheaper and a much more effective use of marketing resources.

In fact, affiliates that put up banners, buttons, and links for the purpose of earning commissions have the added benefit of working to build additional, free awareness too. The Jupiter numbers account only for direct sales stemming from referrals that lead to actual purchases. But, of course, consumers can run across an ad banner for CDnow on AOL.com or another portal site then breeze right by it. Later on, perhaps weeks in the future, when itching to buy a new

CD, the customer could subconsciously remember that ad and proceed right to CDnow's front door. That's known as an "indirect" referral. And if you do count those referrals, Jupiter says, affiliate networks will soon drive the *majority* of online consumer transactions.

Affiliate Abuse

As with most good things, affiliate networks are open to abuse.
And everyone involved—from online merchants, to potential affiliates, to shoppers—should be hypersensitive to the most common
ploys.

Every day an average of 10 new revenue-sharing programs apply for a listing on the Refer-It.com site, a testament to the rapid
growth of these networks as well as the ability of a worthy idea to
mutate in strange ways. James Marciano, who runs the site, typically lists half of them and rejects the other half right away. "We
turn down a lot of stuff that's really schlocky," he says. "We look
for companies that are established and selling their own products."

If a company is not selling its own products or is not even an authorized agent of a bona fide wholesaler, then watch out. Some of
the applicants to Refer-It.com are outright scams in which resellers
of someone else's products are in turn looking to recruit their own
resellers. These have the potential to turn into full-blown pyramids.
In the United States, the Federal Trade Commission and state at-
torneys general police such activity. A sales syndicate is generally
labeled a pyramid if the majority of its sales comes from payments
for recruiting the next layer of resellers. In other words, if the majority of revenue doesn't come from actual product sales, there could
be trouble. Full-blown pyramid schemes can be prosecuted
for fraud.

On the other side of the law, the perfectly legal side, are the
thousands of legit multilevel marketing (MLM) programs. These

have already become a world unto themselves, spawning piles of motivational videos and books. And several programs, such as Amway and Mary Kay, are well known. (Amway boasts 1 million salespeople.) Marciano reluctantly lists some multilevel programs, but instead of placing them into his regular product categories—such as music, food, clothing, travel, software, and sporting goods—they are lumped into a category simply called MLM. Marciano calls this the "cesspool" and the "garbage dump" of his site. And he says he has a category for them only to reduce the number of complaints he gets from those programs he rejects outright.

The difference between an MLM and an online affiliate network should be clear. Under an MLM, resellers generally have incentives to go out and recruit other resellers who recruit more resellers and so on. Sellers on the top levels can collect handsome commissions from the people on the levels below them. The more people working under them, the more they make. In a Web-based affiliate program, there should only be *one level*. If you are joining an affiliate program and commissions are offered for you to sign up other resellers, that should be a red flag. The purpose of any quality affiliate program should be to sell products and services, not to get affiliates to sign up even more affiliates.

If you think about it, there is no reason for these networks to have more than one level. Why would you need a website for recruiting affiliates for someone else? If someone wanted to join, say, the Amazon.com Associates Program, he could simply go to the Amazon site himself. MLM programs are based on geography and acquaintances, recruiting and training people you know or who live near you. On the Web, every site is a click away from all the others.

Another questionable scheme, according to Marciano, is so-called mirroring. When mirroring someone else's website, people just save the graphics and text on someone else's website, copy it onto their own hard drive, and upload it to their own Web address. This is a useful practice in the event that a certain site is completely overrun with traffic. When the Heaven's Gate cult site was in the news a few years ago and getting millions of hits per minute, many news organizations mirrored the site on their own servers. This way more people were able to see it. And since those guys were already dead, they really couldn't complain too much.

But it's not acceptable to mirror a legitimate affiliate program by copying someone else's idea. Sometimes such sites are hard to detect because the scammer will simply change the brand name or superficially disguise the copied site. Marciano looks out for this. Even sites that copy or seem to copy the main features and product mix of a legit player are in danger of being rejected.

There is another, even more subtle loophole in most affiliate networks. A growing number of affiliates are discovering that if they click through their own sites to shop at, say, Amazon.com or CDnow, they can collect commissions on their *own* purchase. As a result, you can conceivably get the typical 40 percent off the price of a new hardcover book, plus an additional 15 percent paid back to yourself as a commission. There is little chance that the merchant could ever break even on such a sale. The worst part is that this subverts the program's original intended purpose, which is to land new customers. Instead, "it becomes a loyalty shopping program in disguise," says Marciano.

Shawn Haynes of Amazon.com says that using your own associates site for your own personal shopping is a violation of the agreement that every new member must click "yes" to before joining. He calls this a form of abuse and says that Amazon has kicked some associates out of the program for doing this way too much.

But in general, this form of abuse is difficult to detect, as these kinds of transactions are growing too fast for humans to ferret out. Haynes says Amazon cannot possibly police every transaction. In the future, the software should simply be able to detect whether legitimate commission does or doesn't apply to that transaction.

In the meantime, Marciano expects this problem to get even

worse before it is fixed. It's a living example of how para-sites can eat away at, and eventually destroy, the host. What happens, for instance, if an online book merchant decided to introduce a loyalty program offering, say, 10 percent discounts to program participants as well to frequent shoppers? Then the customers could conceivably get the original 40 percent, the 15 percent commission, plus an additional 10 percent off. "This is a real dilemma," Marciano says.

Some of these marketing concepts are so original and clever that one feels like standing up and giving a round of applause. For a limited time, a travel site called travelzoo.com promised that people who signed up would be granted three shares of stock in the company. After providing their name and e-mail address, applicants were e-mailed back a message that lists the "registration numbers" on the shares that they now owned. If these new shareholders then encouraged someone new to join, they were granted additional shares up to a maximum of ten. The company claimed to have limited the number of such shareholders to 700,000 and to have given away more than 2.7 million shares, or 27 percent of the company.

If the company one day goes public, TravelZoo implied, the shares could potentially be worth a considerable amount of money. "This would be a sensation in the world of finance," TravelZoo founder and CEO Ralph Bartel told me. "No company has ever given out so many shares before. No one paid anything for them! So let's see if everybody is lucky and makes some money."

To unravel what is going on here, we have to understand a little about how TravelZoo operates. Bartel, a former journalist from Germany armed with a degree in finance, set up the company as headquartered in the Bahamas. The reason: In the United States you have to issue actual share certificates, he says, and in the Bahamas you don't. The printing and mailing costs of doing so would have exceeded $1 million, Bartel says.

Bartel then set up a subsidiary in Mountain View, California, called travelzoo.com Sales, where he works along with a tiny staff. The

TravelZoo site itself is hosted by a company in Texas. And it doesn't really provide its own travel services. It merely gathers and republishes information—special deals on airfares and cruises and the like—with links to other travel sites. Any revenue that Bartel earns by selling advertising or from commissions collected from linking visitors over to major travel sites such as Preview Travel and Hertz are paid back to the parent corporation in the Bahamas. Bartel has published unaudited quarterly financial statements and has even held an online election to install several shareholders to TravelZoo's board of directors. "The concept," he admits, "is a little complicated to understand."

What could possibly be wrong with this scenario? No one is paying anything, right? There is a hidden cost, however. The whole enterprise is potentially a colossal waste of valuable time and a diversion of valuable attention from the sites set up by its shareholders. During the giveaway period, many shareholders promoted the TravelZoo site on their own home pages in order to obtain more stock. In addition, some shareholders sent out bulk spam e-mail with the hope of landing new recruits—even though Bartel says he strongly discourages shareholders from sending out anonymous e-mail. As a result, traffic rose to 1.7 million visitors per month. "It was a good, inexpensive way to increase our traffic quickly," Bartel says.

In this sense, the shareholders are acting like unpaid affiliate marketers. "Tell all your friends about this!" Bartel wrote in an e-mail to shareholders. "The faster our company grows, the earlier we can think about going public. More "hits," more business for our company!"

Who knows: the TravelZoo site may one day evolve into a successful, profitable venture. Bartel may not have actually harmed anyone in the process. But as these kinds of online marketing concepts proliferate, entrepreneurs and casual Web surfers should keep this in mind: If your time and attention are so valuable to someone else, shouldn't it be valuable to you too?

Who Will Prevail?

The world of affiliate networks has become a Darwinian universe of its own. The fittest programs are driving rapid revenue growth. Thousands of new ones are proliferating constantly. And more and more are just dying out.

Clearly, some products and services are more conducive to forming the core of thriving affiliate networks. Books and CDs obviously work well, in part because of the wide selection. Millions of people define who they are, in part, by declaring which authors or musical artists they like. A person who visits a Green Day site is going to have a totally different psychographic profile than someone who visits a fan site for Celine Dion. That's the key: The products that can benefit most from affiliate referrals are the ones with depth and variety—ones that lend themselves to being put into context for specific target audiences.

Some categories that fit the bill may be surprising. Many online dating and matchmaking services, for instance, go so far as to offer their affiliates a share of all the money earned for the life of the customer. In its first two years in business, the Dallas-based One and Only Personals site, for instance, attracted more than a quarter of a million members, many with full profiles and photographs, as well as 30,000 affiliates, says marketing director Lisa Kohring. The program offers 20 percent commissions on all membership fees and future renewal fees. (It costs $14.95 to join for a month and $79.95 for a year.)

Thus, affiliates have incentive to recruit the world's biggest losers. The longer the member stays with the dating service, the more money the affiliate makes. The program has worked well because affiliates have been target marketing slices of the master database to select groups, creating Jewish singles sites, Bay Area singles sites, divorcee sites, senior citizen sites, disabled people sites, and so on. Often an affiliate's site appears to be its own proprietary online dating service, with its own brand name. But it will also say on the home page that it is part of the One and Only Associates Network.

Other categories of products and services with successful affiliate networks include art, financial services such as online currency exchanges, as well as flowers, food and wine, office supplies, real estate, software, sports, travel, even website design and hosting. If something is being sold on the Web, an affiliate network probably has grown up around it.

What other specific qualities separate the successful programs in these categories from the failures? First, it's vital that Web merchants work to build their brand names on their own, not just rely on their affiliates to spread the word. Amazon.com, Barnes & Noble, CDnow, and CBS Sportsline, for instance, have worked to receive press attention and have spent considerable amounts of money advertising in the mass media. Obviously, it helps to be perceived as a leader in your category. Second, the best affiliate networks have ongoing relationships with their partners, working to provide them with exclusive content, marketing support, timely reports, and timely payments.

Some Web commerce sites would do well to rein in their affiliate programs, close loopholes such as the ability to do personal shopping, and exert more control over the quality of their affiliates. Instead of granting exclusive franchises based on physical locations, as franchise operations do, perhaps they could be granted based on subject-matter territories. With new affiliate networks cropping up at a blazing rate, each network will have to come up with new strategies and new incentives in order to prevail in the marketplace.

Germ Warfare

Hot ideas, images, jokes, and brand imagery can whip around the Web at blinding speeds, taking on a life of their own and start spreading through the culture at large. Affiliate networks are just one low-cost way of spreading your marketing message. But there are other ways.

One alternative example comes from the graphics design company Autodesk Corp., which created a cute little dancing baby image. Autodesk programmers just did it on a lark, but people immediately took to it. These short animation sequences featuring the pudgy, diapered character were e-mailed and replicated all over the Web within weeks. Finally, somehow, the dancing baby ended up with a starring role on *Ally McBeal*, the hot Fox TV series, as well as a spot on some major TV commercials.

But as the dancing baby spread, Autodesk was able to control its proliferation and develop dozens of licensed products. The software that embodies original characters such as this should contain copyright information that establishes the ownership rights of its creator. While most companies aren't as sophisticated as Autodesk in this realm, the spread of cultural icons is a big business that can lead to big profits if something really takes off.

That's why a start-up called Thingworld.com (formerly Parable Corp.) aims to assist, capitalizing on the Web's natural tendency to replicate all of this intellectual property. Based in Newton, Massachusetts, Thingworld.com was launched in 1996 by two former Lotus Development executives. The company's software enables entertainment companies to create animated, talking musical icons, such as flashing logos and jumping characters, and build in the necessary copyright information and hyperlinks. "The Web was built on stealing," says Andrew Collins, Thingworld's vice president of business development. "We're enabling people to steal things in a controlled way so that these things can proliferate."

Call it viral marketing. Or germ warfare. The idea is to create something so cool that others will gladly spread the word. Once a catchy message is released into the online culture, it will grow organically, become contagious, and procreate like pachysandra.

One of Thingworld's clients is Viacom's Comedy Central cable network, which found that thousands of renegade fan sites had stolen copies of its South Park graphic characters from the official site and pasted them on their own. With Thingworld's software, Comedy Central programmed copyright information and hyperlinks into South Park's characters, thus protecting their ownership rights. Now if they are "stolen," the fat chef character and the South Park kids are simple, 28-kilobyte icons that point people back to the main site to view program information and buy T-shirts and other licensed products. The characters can been seen at thousands of fan sites, in a way that pleases both the fans and the company.

Collins says that South Park's ability "to tap organically into its fan base" is one reason why it became the highest-rated show on its network, spawned a cult phenomenon, sold millions of licensed T-shirts, and propelled the characters onto the cover of *Newsweek* after airing its first 10 episodes. "It was partially because of the Web," he says.

Hundreds of other examples of what Thingworld calls "things" reside at its website. Among them are graphic Monopoly tokens, sports team emblems, and branded soda bottles. Traditionally, corporations and sports franchises that owned such valuable imagery would saddle up the lawyers and go to battle against people who infringed on their copyrights. Paramount, for instance, made the obvious mistake of trying to shut down unauthorized Star Trek sites—until it later realized that free hyperlinks that led to merchandise sales are a good thing. "You don't want to spurn your biggest fans," Collins says. "You want to embrace them."

This type of viral marketing has a lot in common with affiliate networks. In the future, companies will want to combine the two. If you provide the things—the dancing, singing, multimedia icons of our age—fans of certain products, companies, TV shows, artists, books, and sports teams will do your marketing for you. For certain products you'll have to pay a commission—either in money or in free merchandise. For others you'll just have to get out of the way and let the proliferation begin. It's a new form of low-cost distribution that builds your brand and increases sales at the same time.

EXECUTIVE SURVIVAL GUIDE:
AFFILIATE MARKETING

▶ The Web is too vast and competitive for you to be able to build your brand on your own and successfully market all by yourself. Recruit affiliate partners to sell your products and spread your marketing message to the far corners of cyberspace. Offer your partners generous commissions for referring potential customers who end up buying from you.

▶ Listing products and linking to them is not enough. Encourage your affiliate partners to add their own value by putting a certain subset of your products and services in a unique informational context for their specific audience.

▶ As competing affiliate networks crop up, aggressively evolve your program, boosting your commissions or offering special deals to your most successful partners. All the while, make sure that you understand the business motivations of your partners—otherwise they may work to undermine your program or defect to a rival network.

▶ Prospective affiliates should be on the lookout for potential scams, such as marketers who do not actually sell their own products and services.

▶ Take advantage of "viral marketing," the Web's ability to spread ideas quickly and cheaply. Encourage your biggest fans and most loyal customers to post your logos, icons, characters, and other intellectual property on their sites, provided that such material always includes official copyright information and links back to your site.

CREATE VALUABLE BUNDLES OF INFORMATION AND SERVICES

Turning Surfers into Subscribers

Neil F. Budde had only one goal in mind: Find the right people and make them pay. Stocky, bearded, easygoing, and talkative, Budde was a veteran journalist and manager with Dow Jones & Company in 1993 when he requested to be put in charge of setting the company's crown jewel property, the *Wall Street Journal,* on the Internet. In stark contrast to other newspapers and media companies going digital at the time, the initial aim wasn't just to shovel print content online and then watch what happened. Neither was the objective to rely solely on potential online advertising revenue as a way to cover the operation's costs. Rather, the original mission, Budde recalls, was "to turn surfers into subscribers."

Given the nature of the Internet itself, it was far from clear how his goal could be accomplished. Back then, virtually everything online was free. Free information had long been embedded into the culture of the Internet, going back to the days when it was the province of government researchers, techies, and students. Now, with the amount of no-cost news and information expanding at such a prodigious rate, it was entirely possible that charging would be out of the question. "We knew that a certain segment of the Net population wouldn't pay for anything on principle," Budde recalls.

Meanwhile, established business models didn't work. Dow Jones had long been in the business of charging high access fees for business and financial information, competing with Lexis/Nexis and others in that market. Corporate users had been paying per-minute usage rates to retrieve news articles and business reports. Along those lines, Budde attempted to levy 50 cents per minute for access to the *Journal*'s online Money & Investments section. Users balked at the idea of having a meter running. The effort ended quickly and badly.

By the spring of 1996, around the time he turned 40, Budde had a new plan. He would let visitors use the site for free, but only if they registered, sending in their name, address, and e-mail address. They would also be informed that this was a six-month trial period only and that it would cost real money after that ($49 per year, or $29 for current print subscribers). About 650,000 people registered. It seemed promising.

But it was also frightening for Budde and his growing staff at the *Journal*'s expanded Interactive Edition. What if nearly everyone refused to give up their credit card numbers when the time came? Budde had hired dozens of journalists, programmers, and designers, moving them into a high-tech newsroom on the ninth floor of Dow Jones' offices in the World Financial Center at the business end of Manhattan. There was a lot riding on the outcome: If it turned out that there weren't enough subscribers to cover the operation's costs, would the staff be let go? Would they be able to find jobs elsewhere in the company?

To ease the transition to an all-paid site, Budde signed a deal with Microsoft, under which new users of Microsoft's Internet Explorer browser would obtain a free trial subscription for three months. "Microsoft paid us for the next bulk of users," he says. Then, when it finally came time for everyone to pay for themselves, in January 1997, the site had secured nearly 50,000 credit card numbers. It might sound embarrassingly low for the largest national newspaper, one with a daily circulation of nearly 2 million. But it was a start, a base to build on. The hiring continued, and the staff grew to 100 full-time employees.

These early experiences led to the first lesson in generating revenue from subscribers: Sellers of digital products and services must first create at least *the perception of value* in the marketplace. Even though the *Interactive Journal* was free at first, Budde made it clear that it was worth a certain price. When you know something costs money, it naturally seems worth more than something you get for nothing. The audience had this response: Since we're going to pay for it, we want to use it as much as possible to get our money's worth.

This is not the only way to create perceived value. This quality also can derive from feelings of mass popularity—if millions of other people seem to like it. That, for example, is how Yahoo gained the perception of value. It gave away its product for free at an opportune time, before there were any other Web directories established in the market. It suddenly found itself at the center of a vortex of press, investor, and user attention. But as more and more people try to copy Yahoo's strategy, it becomes less and less effective. Now it's almost impossible to launch successful new Web directories. Attention vortexes on the Web have tended to form around companies that create entirely new categories.

By contrast, the *Journal* was already in an established market— financial news and information—and so the possibility of giving it away for free and establishing a brand-new category was not there. So Budde tried the alternative. When everyone else zigged, he zagged.

The subscription base for the *Interactive Journal* quickly soared past 100,000. But when it came time for the first batch of annual renewals, Budde's staff once again felt a sense of dread. They all knew that a year is an eternity on the Web. There were tons of new competitors dispensing interactive investment services plus free business news and financial advice. What if we were wrong? they thought. What if most subscribers fail to renew and just let their subscriptions lapse?

The Value Bundle

To head off such a scenario, Budde's staff developed and introduced a rapid barrage of new interactive services. They expanded the on-line stock tracking feature, in which users keep tabs on their holdings and fantasy stocks, from one portfolio to five. They added the full contents of sister publication *Barron's*. They created a special Tech Center, consolidating all high-tech coverage in one place. They enhanced the Personal Journal, the section of the site that collects only stories that contain key words selected by the user. They provided real-time stock quotes instead of those at a 15-minute delay. They added the ability to create custom graphs and charts for any stock or security.

The site now contained scores of interactive services and places to go. Other sites also had constant market updates and many of these other features. But now subscribers didn't have to look elsewhere. They could get it all at one spot.

"You can't stand still," Budde says. "We are constantly asking: Is there enough value? The newspaper alone doesn't just translate over to the Web. There has to be much more value. It's a question of creating a valuable bundle that someone else cannot possibly duplicate and give away for free."

The concept of a bundle of valuable products and services, all for one price, proved to be the survival strategy for which Budde was searching. The *Interactive Journal* site managed to retain nearly 80 percent of its first-year subscribers. By contrast, that percentage is usually below 50 percent for most print magazines that ask for renewals by mail. To celebrate their early success, Budde threw a staff party at a local pool hall.

Since then the *Interactive Journal* has maintained this lofty renewal rate. But there was an additional reason why the renewal rate has remained so high, although it may seem counterintuitive. The *Interactive Journal*'s registration process, Budde now admits, was cumbersome—very poorly designed, with too many screens and steps. After expending so much effort getting through it, readers tended to stay committed. "People feel that they've invested so much time into it that they don't drop out," Budde jokes. He has since streamlined the process. In addition, subscribers no longer have to enter a password. Provided you use the same computer, the site will recognize your "cookie," the piece of code on your hard drive that helps the site remember who you are, and log you in automatically.

The business model began to make financial sense when the *Interactive Journal* finally hit 200,000 paying subscribers. Two-thirds of the subscribers were online only, while the other third also received the paper edition. That meant that the average annual rate was $40 each, which works out to more than $8 million in revenue. The revenue breakdown, according to Budde, comes out to 40 percent from subscription fees, 10 percent from premium services, and 50 percent from advertising.

Budde says it's best not to depend on advertising for all of one's revenue, at least in his case. Notoriously rising and falling with the state of the economy, "the ad market can come and go," he says. Even in the best of times, "there is still a huge glut of unsold ad space on the Web." Paid subscribers are more desirable for advertisers anyway, as marketers would rather reach a committed audience that visits repeatedly. His online subscribers visit once every three days—spending an average of about three hours there per month, compared to just 19.5 minutes per month by the average visitor to the free site of the *New York Times.*

Loyal subscribers also tend to buy extra goodies. Since certain services are used only sporadically or by a small percentage of users, Budde has placed such offerings outside the bundle. For instance, readers can obtain stories from the paper's deep archive for $2.95 a pop. Newer premium services include daily video footage of market-moving events and interviews with CEOs for an extra $7.95 per month; personalized, one-on-one career counseling for as much as $279 per session; and analyst reports from top securities firms for $10 each.

Besides, he admits, the so-called click-through rates for ads in the *Interactive Journal* are abysmally low, in the range of 1 percent. That's become par for the course on the Web. But it means that 99 percent of people who see a given online ad banner or button are not interested enough to click on it to learn more. At a typical cost of $65 per 1,000 readers, the ad banners can seem quite expensive, on the order of $50,000 per month. One must be realistic about the value such ads deliver: If they only attract a few hundred people, then are they really worth it? If too many advertisers start asking that question, the already lackluster Web advertising marketplace could dry up. And having a paying subscriber base can cushion any such downturn.

The total cost of producing the *Interactive Journal* has been running at slightly more than $20 million annually, not including the shared resources such as infrastructure and accounting that have been borrowed from the parent organization. That put the operation at close to breaking even by 1998. Budde says that operating profits should begin to flow starting in 1999.

How do the costs compare with the print version? Out of the typical $175 that print subscribers pay, $100 goes for newsprint, ink, and distribution. But the paper edition brings in about $500 in revenue per subscriber, mostly from advertising. The *Interactive Journal,* by contrast, may be much cheaper to produce, costing only a few dollars annually per subscriber to create and post online. But the revenue is much lower right now too, only approaching $100 per paying subscriber, mainly because rich advertising dollars simply aren't available online.

The real payoff from creating a value bundle comes when the subscription base starts to get much larger. With a relatively stable set of fixed costs (employees, technology, etc.) and almost no variable costs (printing and distribution of extra copies are virtually free), the *Interactive Journal* could become a hugely valuable and profitable property as its subscriber base approaches 1 million, a level not unreasonable when you consider Budde's aggressive plans for international expansion.

Could the *Interactive Journal* become too successful? So far, says Budde, the company hasn't detected a significant number of print readers who cancel their subscription because they want to move to online only. Most people who sign up for the Web edition are totally new or are "recaptured" readers who had previously canceled the paper for various reasons. (Rural readers, for instance, can't get it delivered first thing in the morning and must wait for the mail carrier.) During all this time, the paper's circulation base actually has increased slightly. But as the interactive base grows, encroachment may be inevitable. "Where is the inflection point where we begin to cannibalize print?" he asks.

The answer is unclear. However, no one doubts that the print edition that is cranked out by colossal, noisy machines will be around for a long time, perhaps forever. Budde has already learned of strange behavior indicating that many people do indeed want both. Some readers see articles of vital interest in the print edition and, instead of tearing them out, sit down at their PCs and print out the online version. It may seem silly, but some people like it that way.

To generate even more paid subscribers, Budde more recently launched a substantial free area of the site, with the intention of giving surfers a taste and then luring them in as people who pay. At the same time, he dared to hike the annual subscription price, to $59—a gutsy gamble in a world where almost everything is still free.

How much does the powerful *Journal* franchise have to do with its online success? "No question, we would have far fewer subscribers if we were doing this without our brand name," Budde says. But the *Interactive Journal*'s achievements have been neither anomalous nor predestined. Other companies in a variety of other industries can mimic this success story. By creating and charging for a value bundle, the attention problem that plagues most Web ventures shifts to your favor. "Having all-free content can be a real liability," Budde concludes, "because readers don't have a financial incentive to come back again and again." When it's done right, value bundling secures loyalty, stability, and staying power.

The Webonomics of Bundling

On a chilly Thursday in February, Neil Budde flew to Boston to speak at a class on electronic commerce at MIT. The professor teaching that class had flown in that morning too. Erik Brynjolfsson, an associate professor of information technology, was on leave for a year at Stanford University. But MIT was still making him traverse the continent every week so he could lead this one Thursday afternoon session. So much for the Internet spelling the death of distance.

Tall and thin, Brynjolfsson is a young and rising academic star who gets genuinely excited over what's happening in the world of e-commerce. Budde's talk to the class fit right in with the main focus of the professor's research, which has been on the economic effects of bundling information-based products and services. A main thesis of his is that selling bundles of information goods in large aggregates at a single price will earn higher profits than selling those items separately at separate prices. While Budde's presentation to the class showed how information bundling is working for Dow Jones, Brynjolfsson's research has shown how it can work for many other businesses too.

First, though, companies must appreciate the grand sweep of the theory: "Profitability is maximized by providing the maximum number of goods to the maximum number of consumers for the maximum amount of time," Brynjolfsson and colleague Yannis Bakos write.

There are some obvious examples of this. Some people subscribe to America Online primarily for the e-mail, some for news, some for stock quotes, some for chat, some for travel reservations, some for one of hundreds of other services. "It is unlikely that a single person has a very high value for every single good offered," the professors note. "Instead most consumers will have high values for some goods and low values for other goods, leading to moderate values overall." And AOL's price for this bundle of thousands of information goods and services, at about $22 per month, is certainly moderate.

This bundling strategy works best for information-based products and services that can be delivered over networks. Since digital technology enables the making of perfect copies of, say, an online newspaper at zero incremental cost, companies can package more and more of these digital items into the bundle without incurring additional expenses. This is not true in the physical world, where the cost of printing, distributing, and delivering a newspaper or even a pencil is high enough to prevent giving away the paper or the pencil for free. "This strategy has implications for information goods that are not common in the world of physical goods," says Brynjolfsson.

Consider Maxwell Smart's shoe phone. Although this low-tech/high-tech product seemed darn clever on TV, especially in the 1960s, there is a reason why the shoe phone has never caught on, and it has more to do with the cost than it does with the concept. The cost of bundling a phone into a shoe is significant. You can't produce a shoe phone for the same price as you produce the shoe alone.

"Now consider two information goods, say, a news article and a music video, and suppose that each is valued by consumers between zero and $1," the professors continue. For the seller, adding the online video to the bundle costs nothing at all—given that the video is already produced and that there is no plastic cassette. When the two items are bundled together for, say, $1, some consumers would have previously paid $2 and think it quite a bargain. Others would still think it's worth nothing at all to them.

But just like on any bell curve, most customers in the target market would fall onto the high hump in the middle. The $1 bundle price represents the average of the separate price ranges—it is the mean of each of the separate "demand curves" that economists enjoy talking about so much. Most important, selling the two items for $1 will bring in more money than selling the two items separately, simply because it combines two purchasing decisions into one and makes it easier for customers to make the leap toward buying. It maximizes revenue at the same time it reduces the risk that the customers will buy nothing at all.

Now consider selling a bundle of 20 goods for a single price of $10, with each item valued at between zero and $1. In general, the greater the number of items in the bundle, the greater the chances that almost all consumers will find it worthwhile to purchase the entire bundle at the mean value of all the collected items. "The seller will earn higher profits by selling a single bundle of 20 goods than by selling each of the 20 goods separately." The trick is to add enough value to the overall package so that consumers are willing to pay the asking price, but at the same time not include too many items that you could charge even higher amounts for if they were sold separately.

But one thing you should not worry about is including something in the bundle that some customers do not want at all. That's where the research of Brynjolfsson and Bakos has turned up something unexpected. The surprising thing is that this strategy works best if the demand for each of the bundled items is unrelated to one another or even inversely correlated. In other words, the audience that values AOL's financial features and the audience that values its interactive games for kids might have little or no overlap. Most users may not access most of the services. Yet it still makes sense to bundle all of them together.

If you look at AOL as a value bundle, you can better understand its perplexing success. In the fall of 1996, when America Online had just surpassed the 5-million membership mark, the company seemed to hit a wall. Users were greeted with busy signals when dialing into the network. And the ones who managed to get online were encountering painfully slow response times. Analysts predicted that masses of consumers would throw up their hands and switch to rival services. Mary Modahl, of Forrester Research, forecast zero growth in AOL membership. In fact, she said, membership would decline as AOL works through these troubles.

But within the next year, AOL's membership more than doubled, to nearly 12 million. "I was absolutely wrong," Modahl later said. What she and others underestimated was the power that value bundling has to lock in consumers. After all, this is where their e-mail was being delivered. For most consumers, the hassle of learning to navigate a new bundle of services and tell everyone about their new address exceeds any benefits of switching.

The experiences of AOL and the *Interactive Journal* are consistent with Brynjolffson's findings. And it's the sheer unpredictability of Web commerce that makes the strategy particularly compelling. Many competing companies are blazing new territory. And the market changes too quickly to be able to forecast demand accurately. Value bundling, at bottom, is based on probability. It actually takes advantage of the uncertainty of consumer behavior.

"Consumer valuations for a stock quotation service, an on-line sports scoreboard, a news service, or a piece of software will vary," the professors write. Sometimes they will vary widely and independently of one another. However, if all these items and more get packaged together, the probability that a consumer will have a strong opinion on whether to buy the bundle or not is much lower. "The more goods included in the bundle, the less likely it is that any given consumer's valuation for the entire bundle will be very low or very high."

Value bundling works for the very same reason that a Standard & Poor's (S&P) 500 index fund is almost always the best investment choice. Despite attempts by the most brilliant investment minds to hand-pick a winning portfolio, the unmanaged S&P index fund consistently beats 90 percent of all mutual funds year after year. It works so well because the market is unpredictable. Instead of predicting what will perform best, it bundles the risk and rewards into a single package.

And like a mutual fund, value bundling works best over long periods of time rather than short ones. Give the customers long-term access to the bundle—because there are times of the year that they won't use it at all. Health clubs are analogous because, like websites, they also do not incur additional costs when a new member joins. Most health-club memberships are renewed annually, and this is a more profitable way to charge than per visit. The rule of thumb is that 40 percent of health-club members never show up in a given month, and many people never come at all during the summer. For the same reason, an annual subscription to an online encyclopedia or an online sports information site will be more profitable than charging by the month, the professors say.

Still, relatively few companies have tried to create significant bundles and charge for them. Many of those who ignore this strategy will be starving themselves of a key source of revenue, perhaps needlessly. Meanwhile, the companies that execute it successfully, such as the *Interactive Journal,* are bound to dominate their markets and become the 500-pound gorillas of the digital landscape.

Dangerous Bundle or Innovative Integration?

When a company with monopoly power embraces the value bundling strategy, it can be downright dangerous to its competitors. "We find that in a variety of circumstances, a multiproduct monopolist will extract substantially higher profits by offering a single bundle of information goods," the MIT professors write.

The most conspicuous case of winner-take-all bundling involves none other than Microsoft. In general, there is nothing wrong with combining previously separate products into one package. Indeed, if there is added value for the customers, or if the bundled products are more useful working together than they were on their own, then it becomes almost impossible to argue against the practice. But because of Microsoft's unique position, it has taken much heat for doing just that.

One classic case of such aggregation is the software bundles of five or more PC applications such as spreadsheet, word processing, presentation graphics, database, and scheduling programs. Back in the old days, the 1980s, Lotus Development used to sell its market-leading 1–2–3 spreadsheet program for more than $500. But by 1992, as the market grew more competitive, it was bundling nearly $2,000 worth of programs together into its new SmartSuite and selling the bundle for a mere $300. Microsoft, of course, was doing the same and soon saw even greater success because its programs seemed better tailored to new versions of its Windows operating system. WordPerfect, then the market leader in word processing, followed by assembling its own bundle with partners such as Borland, Novell, and later Corel.

The programs weren't just slapped together. They were able to swap data and often shared common utilities, such as spell checkers and graphics tools. They were "integrated." These lower-cost software bundles greatly increased demand for all application software. Even if you didn't use the spreadsheet at all, it made sense to buy the bundle. Application bundles became a must-have at the same time that the global installed base of PCs jumped from tens of millions to hundreds of millions.

Then these software bundles entered their inevitable incarnation as pure digital products. It no longer made sense to sell big boxes with disks and manuals in stores. When software bundles came loaded onto hard drives, there were no longer any costs associated with supplying extra copies of the bundles or adding more programs to it. The more bundles they sold, the cheaper the per-unit cost became, the lower the bundle price became, leading to sales of more bundles, enabling the supplier to improve the package, which would repeat the cycle over and over.

The law of increasing returns set in. The old saying that "nothing succeeds like success" is especially true with intellectual property such as software, movies, and music. Once a certain title gets over a certain threshold, it often becomes a self-reinforcing runaway bestseller. In the PC applications business, there was an especially strong positive feedback loop. As more and more people became familiar with using Microsoft Office, as more and more files were in its proprietary format, it became an industry standard of sorts.

Then the endgame kicked in. IBM acquired Lotus and included the SmartSuite on its PCs, while Microsoft struck deals with Compaq, Dell, and others to package its Office bundle. Corel WordPerfect, meanwhile, couldn't lock in distribution and keep up with the race to bundle more and more value, so it sold its bundle at a greater discount. By now consumers can purchase an entire application bundle for less than $150 when ordering a new computer. IBM often includes it for no extra charge. Yet despite these dramatically lower prices, Microsoft's revenue and profits on its applications suites are higher than ever.

Microsoft initially got into some trouble for this, as competitors cried foul to federal trustbusters. Rivals alleged that Microsoft had an unbeatable edge in making its programs work best with Windows and that it was "tying" products together, forcing PC makers who licensed Windows to supply only Microsoft's bundle. But because it also could be argued that those competitors—Lotus, Borland, WordPerfect, Novell, and Corel—all were at least trying to use a similar strategy, these charges were excruciatingly hard to prove.

Microsoft got into even more trouble with the Justice Department when it used the bundling technique against its newer rival Netscape. When it bundled Windows 95 together with the Internet Explorer browser and called the resulting product Windows 98, the feds pounced once again, charging that Microsoft was stifling innovation and using its monopoly power to put Netscape out of business.

Ironically, during the investigation and the congressional hearings on the matter, Netscape was beating a quick retreat from the browser wars, reducing its reliance on that product dramatically, from 50 percent of its revenue to zero within a year. Now, once again, it was giving away all copies of its browser away for free and concentrating on corporate applications and extracting sponsorship revenue from its NetCenter hub. Then, during the heat of the court battle, Netscape agreed to become part of AOL and its ever-expanding value bundle.

Netscape knew it was fighting an unwinnable battle. A U.S. Court of Appeals judge had already ruled that the two separate products, Windows 95 and Internet Explorer, could also be viewed as one product. Microsoft, in the view of the judge, had achieved "integration." The court even provided a definition of this kind of value bundle: "a product that combines functionalities in a way that offers advantages unavailable if the functionalities are bought separately and combined by the purchaser."

Whether Microsoft was right or wrong to use this strategy, all value bundlers should use this guide: The combined package must be better than the sum of its parts. Often bundlers can do this by building an intuitive user interface that enables users to jump easily from product to product and use them as if they were one: Click on a company's name in a news story and get a real-time stock quote. Click on the stock quote and get a chart showing the stock's movement over the past year. Click on a button below the chart and get an estimate of future earnings. This way, when you end up in the position of undisputed rulership over your industry, you'll have a neat demo to impress the hell out of the judge.

Bundles, Bundles Everywhere

At first glance, it may seem that value bundles are everywhere. Citicorp merged with the Travelers Group so that it could offer a comprehensive bundle of banking, brokerage, and insurance services. AT&T acquired Tele-Communications Inc. to assemble an integrated package of local, long-distance, Internet, and cable TV. They may or may not succeed in developing truly unique offerings, but at least they are charging for their packages. On the Web itself, the major hub sites such as Yahoo, Lycos, Infoseek, and Excite have been frantically assembling greater and greater value bundles, but they have been slow to develop revenue streams that come from consumers.

Some companies have tried it but have fallen short of the mark. The Mercury Center, from the Silicon Valley newspaper the *San Jose*

Mercury News, had charged a subscription fee of $4.95 per month but had to abandon the access charge when it became clear that they weren't creating an ever-expanding value bundle. It seems they didn't have the resources to keep adding new services, products, and features.

Consumer Reports has fared better on this count. The nonprofit publisher has never accepted advertising, and it has naturally extended that policy to the Web, where it charges $2.95 per month or $24 per year for access to its library of articles that rate products, such as appliances, cars, consumer electronics, and so forth. It even offers unique interactive features, such as worksheets, that enable consumers to, say, calculate the overall cost of various cellular and PCS phone rate plans.

Microsoft's *Slate,* after chickening out of charging for subscriptions back in 1996, finally gave it a shot two years later—only to give up again. At $20 per year, it garnered more than 20,000 paying subscribers at one point. That's way down from the roughly 170,000 monthly visitors who had visited for free. Despite some very useful features—such as daily e-mail summaries of how the big national newspapers are spinning big stories—*Slate* has always been more of a webzine than a value bundle.

Others are doing much more. Walt Disney Co.'s Daily Blast, a paid children's site, has said it's signing up more than 500 new users a day at a price of $39.95 per year. The site aggregates games and fun stuff and changes so often that the money paid is often worth the constant surprise.

Meanwhile, CBS SportsLine and ESPN SportsZone have both assembled comprehensive value bundles of sports information and services. Yes, much of the content is free and supported by advertising. But both sites charge $19.95 per year for access to exclusive member content, such as commentary from brand-name sports columnists, an expansive statistics library, sports almanacs, and memberships in fantasy leagues.

A particularly gutsy attempt to charge for a value bundle comes from TheStreet.com. Launched in 1996 by James J. Cramer, a financial journalist and hedge fund manager, the site charges $100 per year for full access to rapid-fire, hard-hitting, daily analysis of markets and opportunities, plus features such as interactive charts that recommend custom investment portfolios. In the first year of subscriptions, the site drew about 20,000 paid subscribers. Says Cramer: "I want TheStreet.com to be the first paid, hourly magazine, hourly newspaper, whatever, on the Net." The company also draws revenue by syndicating its content out to other sites and print publications.

"On the Internet, freeness rules," writes David Kansas, TheStreet.com's editor and a former reporter for *The Wall Street Journal.* "The concept of getting what you pay for has not had a big following. But investors are beginning to discover that free stuff has its own hidden costs. Crucial information gets handled poorly. Plagiarists, fakers, shills and other such ilk litter the free places."

For all these reasons, the everything-should-be-free mentality of the Web's early years is gradually shifting, as more and more companies attempt to climb up the steep, paid-subscription mountain. What many of them are learning is that you actually have to build the mountain, build the bundle, as you climb.

Of course, there are still those with valuable content that insist on giving it away. Martin Nisenholtz, president of The New York Times Electronic Publishing Division, has been dead set against subscription fees from the start. A big believer in interactive advertising, Nisenholtz has been an industry pioneer since the late 1980s, when he headed up the electronic marketing division of Oglivy & Mather. He was running ad campaigns for clients on the Prodigy service before most of us had ever set foot in cyberspace.

But Nisenholtz's early efforts at the *Times* have been a tad frustrating. Yes, he has successfully leveraged the quality journalism produced by the 1,100 people who work in the famous newsroom in Times Square. His site attracted 4 million registered users in its first four years, and 80 percent of people who go there aren't subscribers to the paper edition. But it isn't working out quite as planned. Advertisers should be flocking to nytimes.com for its upscale audience, but they haven't been. Just like everyone else selling ads on the Web, the *New York Times* has had a significant amount of unsold ad space inventory. "We've been talking about database marketing for years," Nisenholtz says. "Now we can deliver it and not enough companies are buying."

By 1998 it was costing $8 million to run the nytimes.com site, and it was bringing in about $6 million in advertising revenue. That's not too bad. But it's not too good either.

Why not charge a subscription price to help close the gap? "To me, it's binary," Nisenholtz replies. "The advertising model is going to evolve or it isn't."

In all fairness to Nisenholtz, he has never had the budget that Budde had, for staff or for technology. The focus has been maintaining the *Times'* signature quality and credibility. It may have been momentarily shaken when, one Sunday, a group of wily hackers, on a dare, broke into the site, took down the *Times* content, and posted pornography instead. But overall the site has kept to the standard established by the newspaper. "We don't take the A.P. [the Associated Press newswire] and call it the *New York Times,*" Nisenholtz says, taking a jab at the CNN site, which simply provides newswire copy and passes it off as its own. "We call it the A.P."

Often the lightning rod for media critics, the *Times* has to consider the situation carefully whenever it tries to tap a new revenue stream. "We have some real opportunities," he says, "but also some real straightjackets." For instance, the decision by the *Times* to link its book review section to Barnes & Noble and earn affiliate commissions was widely controversial, especially among employees and independent bookstore owners. But he notes that the reviews are always written honestly and not with boosting book sales in mind.

For Nisenholtz, the bottom line is this: You cannot charge for general-interest content on the Web, not when so many rivals provide it for free. The *Wall Street Journal* can do it because it's a financial newspaper, he says. But there has to be a niche. Perhaps he's right. The sites that are successfully charging for value bundles do tend to occupy and dominate unique market positions.

What would be the natural niche for the *Times?* What would be the area where it could create a unique value bundle? The answer was right under their noses and right outside the window: New York City itself. In the fall of 1998, the *Times* debuted an all-new site called nytoday.com. Packed with the latest reviews and previews of local restaurants, theater, music, nightlife, museums, art galleries, books and author appearances, sporting events, neighborhood happenings, and shopping, the site bundles in one place virtually all the entertainment options available in the world's top entertainment city. In addition, it offers personalized services, such as a custom events calendar and e-mail notifications of events that individuals choose to know about.

The *Times* is not yet charging for the service. But it's evolving in the right direction, becoming a unique value bundle. By turning its already extensive coverage of local arts and entertainment into a Web information niche, the *Times* doesn't have to compete with the thousands of sources for global political news. Instead, it competes with three or four other online city guides. That gives it a much greater chance of thriving and even dominating a key market.

The Wild-Card Scenario

What are the best strategies for charging for value bundles: annual subscriptions? monthly service fees? pay per use? Can just any type of company pull off the strategy of bundling large aggregates of valuable products and services? Or is this simply reserved for a few dominant players?

One wild-card scenario is that some of the Internet service providers (ISPs)—perhaps ones as big as AT&T or MediaOne—will start creating bundles of bundles. Let's say your ISP, instead of charging the typical $20 for unlimited access to the Net, started offering a $25 monthly service that included subscriptions to the *Interactive Journal, The Street,* ESPN SportsZone, the NetMarket wholesale shopping service, and *Consumer Reports.* It could consolidate all access under one single password and provide a special home page where you could visit and customize your bundle as time goes on—adding and dropping the content channels as you like.

Sound familiar? Of course it does. This is essentially how the cable television industry works. None of the cable networks could afford to stay in business if it had to rely on advertising alone. Instead, the cable providers, from TCI to Time Warner, feed each of the basic networks they carry a tiny percentage of each subscriber's monthly access fee. Depending on how popular the channel is, this payment could be anywhere from five cents to a dollar or so a month. It doesn't sound like much. But when you multiply that by 50 million viewers, it's not a bad business at all.

This is already starting to happen, with AT&T's WorldNet beginning to offer the *Interactive Journal* to its subscribers as a premium service, with a small commission going to AT&T. "Rather than the consumer paying us directly, the subscription price will be added to the WorldNet bill." Budde says. "The advantage to the customer is that you don't have to go through full registration on our site."

And if the ISPs don't take the initiative, perhaps the portals will. One could imagine Yahoo or Excite offering a premium package, in which the user chooses from a selection of subscription sites and pays Yahoo or Excite $10 or so per month, depending on what's included in the bundle. The portal, of course, would take a small sales fee out of that each month. It saves the user from completing many different registrations and having many different passwords and monthly bills. Plus, it would finally get revenue flowing from consumers to the popular websites that have been solely dependent on advertising and sponsorship dollars in the past.

This type of bundling system would open up new vistas to all the companies that aim to get paid for their content or services. For instance, what if Amazon.com offered a preferred shoppers club for loyal customers? The service might include special book recommendations, special discounts, or other personalized content and shopping services not available to everyone. It could have the ISP or portal company bundle in a small monthly fee, perhaps as low as 50 cents per month.

In the final analysis, the best way to become a true intellectual property business is to charge people for your intellectual property. If you give all your intellectual property away for free and depend on some other revenue stream, then you may really be in another business entirely.

Amazon, for instance, has really been acting way too much like a retail business, despite its prowess as an innovative developer of software and a clever packager of information about books and CDs. According to Amazon's financial reports, its gross profit margins on books are about 22 percent, meaning it can keep about $4.40 on every $20 sale. The problem with Amazon's business model is that its marketing costs alone have been eating up the entire gross profit on every transaction. Amazon's other overhead costs, including employees, infrastructure, and technology, plus interest on debt, has in the past added up to net losses in the range of 12 percent of revenue. Then, when you add the huge one-time charges of acquiring new companies, you can see why it has been reporting sizable losses.

Adding more and more products to the mix or even selling 10 times more doesn't help this fundamental problem very much. For instance, Amazon says that gross margins on CDs and videos are even lower than those for books. When your gross margins are so slim, there isn't much room for ever making Microsoftian levels of profit. Even Amazon's move to become its own wholesaler doesn't alleviate its profit problem. Wal-mart, for instance, also has gross margins of about 22 percent, and it has to sell $100 billion worth of merchandise to match the net profits that Microsoft makes selling just $10 billion worth of software.

Gross profit margins on selling information services generally range from 60 percent on up. Getting paid for intellectual property as well as physical goods would give online retailers a much better chance at moving out of the red and into the black. Of course, before one begins charging for such services, one must first build the compelling value bundle. But hey, why not try? The best way for many of today's unprofitable Web ventures to endure will be to start acting like the intellectual property companies they really are.

EXECUTIVE SURVIVAL GUIDE:
VALUE BUNDLING

▶ In the hypercompetitive Web world, only the players that aggregate a unique bundle of information and interactive services will be able to charge for access to their content.

▶ By charging for your content, the attention problem that plagues most Web ventures shifts to your favor. When people are paying, they then have a financial incentive to return to your site again and again.

▶ Keep evolving your value bundle, adding new products and features to it at a rapid pace.

▶ The bigger the bundle, the better. Bundles of information goods available at a single price will usually earn higher profits than if those items were sold separately—even if not all customers place a high value on every item in the bundle.

▶ Invent ultra-high-value services and keep them outside the bundle. Offer those to your customer base as premium product, available for an extra fee.

▶ Dominate a niche market. The value bundles that have the best chance of survival are the ones that don't try to be everything to everyone but rather concentrate on a specific subject area with a specialized audience.

SELL CUSTOM-MADE PRODUCTS ONLINE, *THEN* MANUFACTURE THEM

Information Instead of Inventory

On a hot Texas afternoon, an electronic commerce director at Dell Computer Corp. named John Winfrey is driving me to a factory in the north of Austin. As we approach it from the elevated freeway, the white boxy structure looks like a colossal sugar cube. The heavily guarded building, called Metric 12, is ground zero for the new world of "network production." A 33-year-old with a medium build, medium-brown hair, and sporting a medium-brown "Buy-A-Dell" polo shirt, Winfrey explains that Metric 12 is named after a preexisting industrial zone at this location and that no one inside is necessarily measuring motherboards in millimeters.

Before we enter, Winfrey also explains what it means to have worn employee badge number 4,538 for more than six years in a company that now has more than 16,000 such badge numbers. The lower the number, the longer you've been with the company, and the longer you've held Dell stock. Since it began taking custom orders over the Web in 1996, Dell has seen its stock double roughly every six months. Overall, Dell's shares have appreciated more than 30,000-fold since 1990. For many employees, the raging runup has come at a price, with high rates of total burnout and divorce among his colleagues, as Winfrey himself can attest. But the money helps assuage it all. When Michael Dell's 38-year-old secretary suddenly announced her retirement, everyone knew why: low badge number. "I'm now thinking about what I should do with my second life," Winfrey says, as we pull open the thick glass doors.

My camera has to stay in the car or it will be confiscated by security, Winfrey cautions. The guards at the entrance are strict, but not as strict as the ones at the exit, where every employee and visitor must pass through a metal detector and baggage scanner. Since Dell is the top supplier of personal computers to the U.S. government, this factory has been designated a U.S. Customs Subzone. A sign warns that anyone caught with unauthorized equipment or misappropriated material faces "up to a $5,000 fine or a 10-year prison sentence." One visitor remarks: "I'd take the fine."

At the end of a hallway, the factory floor is first visible through a floor-to-ceiling window. Step inside, and steady buzzings, sudden swishings, and the smell of corrugated cardboard fill three football fields of frantic activity. The action begins to the left, where long cargo trucks cozy up to rectangular holes in the wall. Each truck is stocked with a specific part, be it memory modules, microprocessors, power supplies, or computer casings. And Dell does not own or take possession of any of these components until the minute they are ready to be slapped into a system; only then are they physically lifted from the truck and brought to the other side of the wall.

This way Dell doesn't have to pay for the parts before they actually use them. It's the reason that Dell has "a negative cash conversion" of five business days, meaning customers pay Dell for their computers, on average, about a week before the money goes out to the suppliers of parts for those very same computers. It is a corporate accountant's wildest dream.

"We tell our suppliers exactly what our daily production requirements are," Michael Dell told the *Harvard Business Review.* "So it's not, 'Well, every two weeks, deliver 5,000 to this warehouse, and we'll put them on the shelf, and we'll take them off the shelf.' It's 'Tomorrow morning we need 8,562 units, and deliver them to door number seven by 7 A.M.' "

As a result, Dell has developed a trait that eventually will be necessary for all surviving species of manufacturers: the ability to replace inventory with information. The product is produced *virtually* on the network, before it is produced *physically* in the plant. This method of network production will become vital in all manufacturing businesses, but it's already so in the computer business, in which the market value of components and systems has been declining, on average, 1 percent per week. Dell's top 15 suppliers, representing nearly 90 percent of all its procurement, have established direct business-to-business ordering systems over the Internet as well. This way Dell can use the network to specify components over private extranets the same way its customers buy entire systems.

When a custom order comes in for a new system, whether over the Web or over the phone, that order is routed through internal checks and dispatched to the factory floor within a day. Each computer ordered is assigned an asset tag code, such as 63WDC, as well as its own subdirectory on one of Dell's 56 megaservers running the factory. The number will allow customers to "watch" their system being built in real time over the Web, tracking it through an assembly process with seven checkpoints. Afterward, the code becomes their ID for looking up their configuration and the machine's history over the Web as well as for obtaining customer service.

Now, as the assembly process starts here in Metric 12, something unexpected happens. Until this point, almost everything has been managed by machines. But real, live people take over from

here. This may very well be a state-of-the-art factory, but the surprising thing is that there are no robots or robotics in view. Since
every system must be built to order and since this assembly involves intricate turns of small screws, it's all done by hand. It's the
reverse of most modern-day manufacturing. Instead of a labor-
intensive sales process and a machine-intensive manufacturing
process, Dell's system is just the opposite.

An army of workers scampers about the cool cement floor.
Numbering more than 1,200, if you include all the shifts, the
group looks like a cross-section of mall-going America. Every age,
color, and ethnic group is represented. The dress of choice: shorts,
sneakers, T-shirt, baseball cap, safety goggles, and blue wrist bands
that are fastened to something nearby so as to ward off static electricity. You could call this group well grounded.

Indeed, these are the moderate-wage manufacturing workers
that have supposedly vanished from the American economy years
ago. But with a spicy twist: Everyone can participate in the employee stock purchase plan. That's why the fun game around here
is to roam the factory floor in search of low badge numbers. You'll
soon spot some grandma screwing power supplies onto a mother-
board who may very well be a multimillionaire. It's as if everyone
here senses that they could be holding a winning lottery ticket.

Their work is precise. From start to finish, the actual manufacturing process of a computer in Metric 12 takes less than four
hours. That includes the loading onto the hard drive a custom software suite ordered for each machine, plus up to two hours of boot-
ing up, switching off, and other performance tests. This workforce
can do this for more than 7,000 new systems every day.

At all times, the Web is watching them. After employees are
finished with their task—installing the power supply, inserting
memory chips, fitting the hard drive, and so on—they wave a wand
over a bar code stuck to the casing. That transmits a signal to the
bank of central servers. And this information is made available in-

stantly on the Web. That's how customers can track their system being built in real time. If something goes wrong or takes too long, a blue light peering from atop a pole at the end of their assembly line will suddenly start flashing. And a foreman will investigate. Yes, this work can be lucrative, but it's not without its own little pressures.

Stoking Your Business with Bits

The formula for manufacturing used to be fairly straightforward. Ever since Eli Whitney came up with the concept of standardized, interchangeable parts at the dawn of the nineteenth century and Henry Ford's humming assembly lines ushered in the twentieth century, manufacturers have been building their products from start to finish in mass-production factories and shipping them out to wholesalers who would sell to retailers who would sell to customers. Compared to placing custom orders with a lone blacksmith or handicraftsman, the mass-production model was an infinitely more efficient way of getting large quantities of goods to large numbers of people.

Network production combines the best of the two methods: More and more, the future of all manufacturing—from cars, to clothing, to computers, to any other physical good that can be produced—is about getting back to the notion of selling a customized version of your product and *then* manufacturing it. The long-touted concept of "mass customization" is just one of many benefits of network production. The others are: greatly reduced costs and the ability to target market to each customer down the road, selling add-on products, services, and new systems when they are needed. If done right, network production yields efficient manufacturing and unique customer relationships at the same time.

This type of manufacturing has yet to fully penetrate most corporations that make things. Think about all the physical products you buy and how few of them are truly customized. Few manufacturers enable customers to place their orders over the Internet. And even fewer have linked the Web into its central production system.

But the switch should come swiftly. "We're headed to a world of network production in which you've got to be the best at what you do—and only do what you're best at," says Everett Ehrlich, a former chief economist for Unisys and the U.S. Department of Commerce.

This, Ehrlich says, explains the diverging fates of General Motors and Chrysler Corp. Using cheap computer networks, Chrysler had learned that it can send engineering diagrams, product specifications, and production schedules between companies just as easily as within the company. GM, which hadn't yet mastered this type of outsourcing, was hobbled by a brutal labor strike over this very issue at the same time Chrysler was touting its merger with Germany's Daimler-Benz. The vision behind that megadeal is that computer networks enable two engineering teams or two marketing teams in different countries to work as if they were one.

In Brazil, for instance, a small DaimlerChrysler plant that makes pickup trucks uses computer networks to choreograph ordering and production among suppliers, using a manufacturing technique known as modular assembly. When an order comes into the plant for a new truck, DaimlerChrysler immediately relays it to a major supplier's plant two miles down the road. Within less than two hours, the supplier assembles 320 parts—including wheels, axles, brakes, dashboard, and frame—into a chassis that is rolled over to the main plant immediately. There it mates with the engine, transmission, and final fittings. These new DaimlerChrysler assembly lines cost less than $100 million to install, compared to the billion-dollar, monolithic ones that have dominated Detroit for decades. No longer can one company under one roof afford to control the assembly of every part that goes into every car.

By taking apart production that used to happen inside one

factory and parceling it out to computer networks that connect different companies, all the participants can experience high returns on the capital they have invested. The results can be dramatic. The auto industry is now experiencing steady deflation in car and truck prices, yet revenue is increasing. "The rapidly declining cost of information technology is changing the cost structure of firms," Ehrlich says. "Technology obliterates boundaries between companies."

The lesson: your company must develop some set of core capabilities that you can do better than anyone else. And everything else must be subcontracted and produced by teams of companies working together across networks. Dell got where it is because it is the most efficient marketer and assembler of other people's computer and software technology. It uses computer networks to order, coordinate, specify, and deliver its products and services. It relies on Airborne Express and other package delivery companies, for instance, to make sure that the computers it assembles in its own factory are matched up with the correct monitors. Those monitors come from a completely different factory, run by Sony or someone else. But when the two boxes arrive at the customer's doorstep together, the customer won't know or care. That, too, is a form of network production.

This strategy can free a business to enter entirely new markets. After some introspection, The Swatch Group decided that it could evolve into something different from the world's biggest watch company. It could leverage its assembly and design skills in the market for selling alphanumeric pagers. Of course, that also led to the long-time, secret-agent ideal of integrating a telephone into watches. So now it's in the telecommunications business even though Swatch itself doesn't have to know much about telecommunications. Next it's rumored to be entering the car market, as the company is reportedly developing a cute little urban vehicle with a shockingly low price point. But the beauty of it all is that it only has to specify the design and then farm out all production to other firms over a network.

The reason why mass customization hasn't worked very well in the past has to do with the high costs of managing unique customer relationships. In Japan, Toyota salespeople would visit the homes of customers, have tea, and proceed to take down a very personalized order, which would then be handed off to the manufacturing department. A great idea, but so expensive, time-consuming, and cumbersome that Toyota had trouble making any money on such custom orders. It finally phased out the service. The problem seemed to be that the salespeople didn't let customers do enough of the work themselves.

And in the United States, many car makers and dealers have hardly even attempted this. A few years back, I ordered a blue Toyota Corolla wagon from a local dealer. About 10 days later, the dealer called back to tell me that my red Toyota was in. So I drove away in a red Toyota. What's more, it has some options, such as a roof rack, that I had to pay for but didn't want or order. The process hasn't changed much since then. If the dealer doesn't have what you want on the lot, it will simply try to locate a car that closely matches.

In network production, you should be able to get a car built just for you. In a sense, we are resurrecting the blacksmith, reverting back to the strict definition of the sixteenth-century word "manufacture," which derives from the Latin *manu factus,* or made by hand. When mass production became dominant, that original meaning was lost, as manufacturing eventually became something done strictly by machines before the customer was involved.

The world has changed once again: Instead of first making the widget, and then having the customer view widget choices and buy the widget, we're now moving to having the customer design and buy the widget first, and then having you make the widget. The Web itself is forcing this back-to-the-future change upon industry after industry. Only instead of forging iron in a hot fire, lat-ter-day digital craftspeople stoke their business with bits. Instead of deploying more and more sophisticated machines and robotics to churn out masses of identical goods, network production companies differentiate their products with information supplied by the individual customer.

A Bicycle Built for You

Using this method, a startup called Seven Cycles Inc. has suddenly grown to become the largest manufacturer of custom bicycles in the United States. Named after the fact that its seven founders often bike seven days per week, the 12-person company was formed in 1997 with the goal of building a unique bicycle for each rider.

People thought the founders were crazy to produce bikes in America. The United States used to host a huge manufacturing base in the bicycle industry. But now about 95 percent of domestic sales are bikes that are built elsewhere, mainly in China and Taiwan, as mass-manufacturing companies such as Schwinn relocated their factories overseas long ago. The only competitive advantage those manufacturers could think of was lowering their cost of labor.

To get to Seven's factory, you have to ride west from Boston just past Cambridge into an industrial section of Watertown, a densely populated middle- and working-class suburb. The company now occupies the former factory of the Goddess Bra Company, a maker of large-size ladies' undergarments. So instead of middle-age Jewish and Asian immigrant women sitting for hours endlessly sewing the same cloth cups over and over, the 5,000-square-foot space is now staffed with bicycle craftspeople, average age 28, who typically pedal to work and park at a rack inside the front door. The only remnants of the factory's former life are a few leftover photos on the walls—stills from the 1970s of smiling Goddess bra babes with bouffants. "We like to keep that sense of history here," says Rob Vandermark, Seven's CEO, who cofounded the company at age 29.

The factory's main raw materials are lightweight titanium rods, which are delivered through the front door and taken back to three workstations, or "jigs," manned by people named Matt, Skip, and Nancy. Clad in jeans and special glasses, the trio is busily measuring, cutting, fitting, and polishing the silvery rods under bright fluorescent lights. Meanwhile, off to the side is Andy, who may very well be the world's first full-time Webmaster-welder, devoting half his time to each of these jobs. Andy claims that welding the bikes is more difficult than developing Web pages. "I get burned less often when I'm coding HTML," he says.

Each bike comes with a card signed by whoever worked on it, complete with a short bio. These craftspeople are starting to develop a following. "Customers from all over the world will request that Matt must make their frame," Vandermark says, "or that it just must be welded by Tim."

The CEO calls up an incoming order on a computer located in an office just off the factory floor. A woman in Florida named Sandy has just visited the company's website and has sent in specifications for a new touring bike. She's 58 years old, 5-foot-3 inches tall, 113 pounds with a size 7 foot. In all, Sandy has entered about 60 pieces of data, including the length of her arms, thighs, inseams, and shoulders, the measurements of her previous bike, her riding habits, her plans for the new bike, the color she would like, whether she experiences back or neck pain, and how she would like the bike to handle, choosing specific gradations of agility and rigidity. Without the Web and other simple software tools, the company would have a tough time managing all that information.

Only when such orders come in does Seven's staff jump into gear, choosing specific sizes, weights, and frame assemblies in response the order data. "Most companies will estimate demand and build batches of different sizes," says Vandermark, who previously spent 10 years working for a mass-production bike maker that lost money nearly every year. "We make them all one at a time."

The company, however, doesn't sell direct. Even if a customer submits an order over the Web without visiting a local bike shop, as a growing percentage do, they must take their delivery through an authorized dealer. After Seven's first year in business, nearly 100 dealers around the world had officially signed up. And new customers who submit their orders through the Web are constantly recommending new dealers in their area. If customers don't live near a Seven dealer, they can just enter in the name of any local bike shop, and Seven will arrange delivery through that store.

Dealers are necessary, at least for now, because the frames that Seven makes need to get fitted locally with wheels, gears, and handlebars. In addition, all bicycles require regular, on-site service, and customers usually want someone answering questions face to face. "Some people just want their bike as soon as possible," Vandermark says. "But others are really anal and want to go over every detail 20 times."

The company can make and ship a bike in as little as two weeks from when the order is placed. Since titanium rods do not depreciate nearly as fast as computer parts, the company can afford to carry some inventory—usually less than 30 days' worth. But like Dell, Seven Cycles usually receives payment for its products before having to pay for parts that are used to build them.

The market that Seven serves is high end. Its products typically retail for $2,000 and up, with the average price around $4,500. One recent custom order came to $12,000 because the buyer requested that the frame come in several pieces. This way it could come apart easily for packing in an airplane's overhead storage bin. "We're really aiming at the racers, the serious enthusiasts, and other customers with money," Vandermark says.

All told, Seven eked out a small profit in its first full year in business. The company made a total of 700 bike frames and took in about $1 million in revenue, figures that are projected to triple for the following year. "We can't keep up with the demand," Vandermark says. His intermediate-term goal is to ramp the factory up to building 5,000 frames per year, 40 percent going to customers outside the United States. Already the company is granting stock options to its employees with the far-off thought of one day taking the company public.

Seven Cycle's brand of network production offers key lessons in surviving in almost any industry—especially if your industry is dominated by manufactured commodity products but also has an affluent, demanding customer base. Like Seven Cycle, don't make your product until an order comes in for it. Customers actually will pay a premium for a truly customized result. And since they benefit from the transaction, they will gladly hand over data about themselves, establishing a relationship that will most likely lead to additional sales down the road. All businesses should be evolving this way, toward a future of lower costs and more loyal customers.

The Golfer in the Dell

Following Michael Dell's footsteps in launching a new business from a college dorm room are a bunch of Harvard students who started the Chip Shot Golf Corporation. It all began in 1995 when Amar Goel, a kid who grew up in Silicon Valley, decided that he would sell golf clubs over the Web. It was the summer after his freshman year, and it seemed like it would be much more fun than working for someone else. At the time, he thought it was a good business idea for two reasons: First, the demographics of Web surfers and golf players had plenty of overlap. And second, retailers and pro shops tended to overprice their equipment.

Goel then found out the hard way how tricky the business really is. The major brand-name makers of golf clubs, such as King

Cobra and Callaway, set strict suggested retail prices and deal only with authorized resellers and retailers. But since these Harvard kids wanted to sell clubs for less, the manufacturers didn't want to deal with them. "We didn't have accounts with Callaway and the other makers," Goel says. But he did find out that there was a secret gray market in clubs, in which some wholesalers would supply equipment to unauthorized vendors. By obtaining the goods on the sly, Chip Shot Golf could sell clubs for $800 that retailed for $900 or more elsewhere and reach a global base of consumers to boot.

Yet their business model was somewhat of a paradox. "A lot of retailers were getting angry because they were getting beat by these Internet guys," Goel says. "Yet we weren't making much money. It was more hassle than it was worth." He decided that competing on price alone wasn't much of a business model at all. "Any time you compete only on price, someone who sells for $800 will beat someone selling for $800.01. It's a pretty crappy business."

By the time he figured this out, Goel had already recruited two of his classmates from Harvard's golf team and spent a year diverting his attention from what he should have been doing: studying economics. Yet he wouldn't give it up. In retrospect, his idea for reinvigorating the business was an obvious one: They would begin selling custom-built clubs that closely approximated, or "cloned," the performance of the major brands. "We started calling ourselves the Dell of golf," he says.

That too posed a problem. There seemed to be too many ways to customize a golf club. There were 12 gradations of stiffness and flexibility for shafts alone. Then you have to take into account the grip sizes, height, and playing ability of the customer. Just to sell customized versions of a single club would require Chip Shot to carry $4,200 in inventory. "You could have $200,000 in inventory without blinking an eye," Goel says. "We didn't have the capital for that."

That's when the kids followed Dell's lead and decided that they simply wouldn't carry any inventory at all. At the company's website, customers would choose grips, shafts, and club heads tailored to their height, hand size, and playing style. And as soon as a customer's order is received, the company sends it to a local assembly plant already affiliated with existing retailers. The plant makes a set of clubs according to the exact specifications. Chip Shot claims it can have the custom clubs drop-shipped out to the customer within two or three days of taking the order.

The new business model worked. Sales jumped from $121,000 in 1997 to more than $1 million in 1998. Amar Goel started talking the talk of a custom golf club guru: "We wanted to create custom clones of all the popular brands," he rambles. "So we wrote software that asks people questions. We can adjust the lie of the head by two degrees if you want. We can provide people with charts to show what happens if you tend to push the ball to the right. We ask them how long they want their clubs, how often they play, their height, the distance from their wrist to the ground. This is hard and complex. But we can build 150,000 combinations of clubs, and that's growing to 1 million combinations. You can fit everyone out there with those combinations."

After graduating from Harvard, Goel moved the company to the garage of his parents' house in Saratoga, California. It thus became a classic Silicon Valley start-up. The garage held some desks and filing cabinets bought on the cheap at an office supply outlet as well as telephones and computers hooked up to the Internet over a relatively speedy 156-kilobyte digital phone line. In the meantime, he and his colleagues were rejecting offers for real jobs with real companies. "We turned down $70,000-a-year jobs so we could make $1,000 a month."

Goel began pitching the company to venture capitalists, who were predictably eager to fund the start-up. This way, Chip Shot could expand, develop better marketing, and get a real office. After raising $3 million from Sequoia Capital, the firm that originally backed Yahoo, Chip Shot moved into new digs in Sunnyvale and hired more and more employees. It then began spending lavishly on exclusive placement as the only seller of golf clubs on America Online's shopping channel and PointCast's sports channel. The spending put pressure on the company to ramp up sales very quickly or face mounting losses.

The company decided that the target market was the "value golfer," someone who makes under $70,000 per year—not the guy who makes $100,000 and up who probably can afford clubs at an expensive pro shop. He says that Chip Shot still sells for less, only now that isn't its sole advantage. "As a Web company, we don't have 22 percent of our revenue going to overhead," he says. "We have 5 percent, and that's not a matter of belt tightening. It's a radically different model entirely."

Chip Shot is already starting to look like a real company. It started selling custom golf clubs to buyers in dozens of countries, including Australia and Iceland. More recently it launched an affiliate network, paying 20 percent commissions on sales to big and small partners. Goel's near-term goal is $50 million in sales for the year 2000. "Then we have the chance, maybe, to become a $100 million company."

Net Production Pitfalls

There are some potential drawbacks to network production. For instance, if an unhappy customer returns a product, what is one to do with a returned set of one-off golf clubs or a custom bike? If the product cannot be disassembled into its original components, the cost usually must be eaten. In addition, how do manufacturers switch to this model without alienating their existing sales channels and retailers? In the computer industry, "channel strife" is one of the biggest problems faced by Compaq, IBM, and Apple. Some large dealers who have learned that the manufacturer is now selling direct have become so angry that they stopped advertising and recommending that maker's products.

Then there are problems unique to each industry. At conferences in the music business, the talk these days is dominated by the buzzwords of "digital distribution" and "custom-made CDs." Users working at their desks or lounging around the house are already downloading and playing select songs or albums. They are also beginning to choose their own list of songs and have custom CDs manufactured and shipped to them. Inexpensive recordable CD-ROM drives even enable users to download the music and cut their own CDs.

"We're in the very early stages of these technologies," says Debbie Newman, a vice president at Music Boulevard. She says that the big record conglomerates are so far resisting custom CDs, just as they fought unsuccessfully against home taping for years until they realized that taping can help expand the market for their products, not diminish it. But because of the massive copyright issue, the sites that now offer made-to-order CDs often have narrow song selections. "It will be a real market as soon as copyright issues get addressed," Newman says. "It won't replace CDs but rather add another dimension to the business."

Network production has already spread to many other industries, as Web-based companies are already selling made-to-order clothing, fishing rods, and business stationery as well as custom-created vitamin tablets and college textbooks.

But the major economic consequences of this new method will be clear when the world's largest manufacturing conglomerates adopt it. In the future, when shopping for a car, there will be no reason to choose from just the models that currently happen to be in inventory at the dealership or be forced to wait weeks or months while that dealer locates what the customer wants. Instead, customers will log onto the Web or a kiosk at a dealership to select from a far wider range of options, colors, add-ons, and tailor-made features, essentially building their own unique vehicle online.

To accommodate this, car makers will have to completely transform their supply chains and their marketing efforts. In addition, they'll have to retool and perhaps relocate their factories to be closer to the customers. "We're already headed in that direction," says Ehrlich. "The industry has to change its mind-set. Instead of lumping options together and offering products in a limited number of flavors, they will have to sequence their production around what the customer wants."

Highly Evolved Markets

Rivals in the computer business have already received the message, and they are now copying just about everything about Dell's business model. Gateway 2000, which also pioneered the direct sales model, had already been doing much of it for years. But Compaq, IBM, Apple, H-P, and the others had to change in a hurry.

Dell's network production method had yielded profits levels that had been unimaginable for a mere maker of what was thought to be commodity PC clones. Dell's dominance culminated in one 1998 fiscal quarter in which the company made more net profit—more than $500 million—than all other personal computer makers combined. The same thing happened in the quarter after that. And Michael Dell, still in his early 30s, is just getting started despite that fact that he's already the single richest person in the state of Texas—worth at least triple Ross Perot.

Only when the rest of the industry hit this inevitable rough patch of low or no profits did the dark side of Darwinism rear its head. Then the response turned into sheer panic. Compaq, for one, shut down its biggest North American factory completely for two weeks in a desperate attempt to reduce bloated inventories of unsold computers, idling 3,000 workers. To accomplish the same thing, H-P started giving away monitors and printers for free.

They scrambled to begin selling directly over the Web. They installed kiosks at stores such as CompUSA and Circuit City, where customers can configure their own machines and have them shipped to their home. Many of these orders are routed over the Internet to the factories of superdistributors, such as Ingram Micro, which performs the assembly and then ships directly to the customer.

Under this scenario, the manufacturers themselves aren't really manufacturing anything. They are just specifying components, setting prices, and engaging in marketing. And the retailer no longer even touches the finished goods. At Ingram Micro's Memphis factory, all of these brands of PCs are made on the same assembly lines. Only at the end of the line do IBM, Compaq, or H-P casings get fitted.

The big computer makers had no choice in the matter: These computer giants had to adapt to the new environment or they would perish. "Computer inventory is like fresh fish on the table," says Henry Bertolon, CEO of NECX, a Web-based computer and electronics store that sells a variety of built-to-order brands. "It tastes great the first day, but the longer it sits, the smellier it gets."

Still, rivals will find it hard to match Mr. Dell, who by design has no inventory and thus no inventory buildup. By the summer of 1996, Dell was selling an average of $1 million worth of computers online each day, growing to $2 million by early 1997, $3 million by the fall, $6 million per day the following year, and more than $10 million in online sales per day by the following holiday season. Boeing alone purchased more than 100,000 Dell PCs primarily using this direct electronic build-to-order system. And Michael Dell has made it a goal to get half the company's revenue from Web-based sales by 2001. "It's the next best thing to mental telepathy," he has said.

Dell has already whittled down the average time it takes to respond to an order, manufacture the machine, and ship it to that customer's front door to 7 days. By contrast, some of Dell's competitors in PC manufacturing were averaging 38 days to make and ship a machine to their distributors. Under that scheme, retail stores would then hold PCs in inventory for an average of 45 days before selling them. That's a total of 83 days—almost an entire fiscal quarter. Dell found a way to eliminate these enormously expensive inefficiencies and largely skirt the crushing boom-and-bust business cycles that have plagued the PC business for its entire history.

Yet even for all its success, even though Dell runs clockwork factories on American soil, many industry leaders are dismissive of its manufacturing prowess. "Dell is not a manufacturing company," says Larry Ellison, CEO of software maker Oracle Corp. "Their R&D is less than 2 percent of sales. They are simply a distributor for Wintel" (the industry term for the Windows-Intel monopoly). Ellison is absolutely right. But given Dell's incredible growth and profits, so what?

EXECUTIVE SURVIVAL GUIDE:
NETWORK PRODUCTION

▶ Develop an easy-to-use ordering system that lets customers build their own unique product online.

▶ Don't let expensive inventory sit around and depreciate in value. Rather, replace your inventory of mass-produced parts with extensive information about how those parts can be configured into many different product combinations.

▶ Decide what your company does best—be it product design, marketing your brand, or customer service—and make sure no one else performs these core competencies better than you.

▶ Then parcel out the remaining functions over the network to factories all over the world that specialize in assembling specific components or some other task.

▶ Maintain the extensive data that customers send in for future reference. The information will be useful in many ways: It will help customer service personnel troubleshoot any problems; it will allow customers to look up their account history online; it will enable you to better anticipate future purchases and tailor your marketing accordingly.

▶ Finally, consider new areas of growth, expanding into new industries in which your core competencies could give you a competitive edge.

6

ADD NEW VALUE TO TRANSACTIONS BETWEEN BUYERS AND SELLERS

The Food Chain

Mack Tilling didn't start out by saying: Gee, the Internet is here. How can I use it to make gobs of money? Rather, he was trying to solve a real business problem. As director of operations at a California-based chain of brew pubs, he was aggravated by the inefficiencies of buying food. There were too many suppliers to keep track of, with too many different forms and contracts. Their printed price sheets and catalogs were always outdated. Their order-taking systems were unreliable, making it hard to coordinate delivery schedules. Since Tilling couldn't find a way to streamline the process, he set out in 1993 to create one.

Along with colleague Ted Daley, he left the restaurant chain and cofounded Instill Corp., based in Palo Alto. The two developed a simple order entry database that they call the "e•store." Using software installed on PCs or Macintosh, food buyers at restaurants, hotel chains, and corporations could use their modems to dial it up, log on, and visit a single place for browsing electronic catalogs, transmitting orders, receiving invoices, and reconciling purchases. Luckily, the Web came along, and the two transferred their e•store to it in 1997, making the ordering process much simpler for both the company and customers.

Still, while the idea sounded promising, Tilling and Daley's new company lacked a critical mass of real orders to turn this into a successful business. They knew that the guy in the back of a restaurant who needed 500 pounds of cheese, 3 vats of guacamole, 422 cases of tortilla chips, and 6 sides of beef by Thursday wasn't going to troll the Net for food unless he knew it was the ultimate marketplace.

The two founders figured that the buying process was only half the equation. They not only had to make it easier to order the food, they had to give the giant food distributors a reason to hand over all of their information, their price sheets and catalogs and contracts. Without the sellers on board, the buyers wouldn't use the system.

From talking to the distributors, one thing was clear: Reducing costs was the number-one goal. If distributors could eliminate printing paper catalogs, if they could reduce costly errors from mishandled orders, if they could reduce paperwork and processing time, then they just might sign on. Efficient Foodservice Response, a research group, estimated that distributors could save $14 billion a year by raising productivity and decreasing errors. In a low-margin, high-volume business, these efficiencies can be the difference between profitability and losing money.

After testing the new service with Marriott Distribution Services, a major seller of food to hotels and institutional kitchens, Instill's founders were able to boast of a 60 percent drop in ordering errors, leading to a big reduction in processing costs. With Marriott and several other big distributors feeding food data into the system, Instill was able to attract more than 1,000 buyers, including restaurants such as Outback Steakhouse, Taco Bell, and

Pizza Hut, hotel chains such as Ritz-Carlton, and corporate catering departments at firms such as Hewlett-Packard.

Finally, four years after starting the company, the buying and selling began to spiral upward. In 1997 more than $180 million worth of food and supplies were purchased at the e•store, and that exploded to more than $1 billion in sales the following year. The business model was straightforward: Instill would charge a fee to set up each buyer with an account on the network and then charge a flat fee of $2.50 for each order processed. Venture capitalists became giddy over the concept of a true business-to-business application in the Web commerce market, and four firms pumped a total of $18 million into the company.

The potential is indeed huge. Food-service sales accounts for 4 percent of U.S. gross domestic product, and it's an industry that has been slow to adopt high technology. More than $150 billion is spent every year to stock 750,000 food-service outlets in the United States alone. And the 20,000 or so distributors of food products are still relying mostly on paper catalogs, phone calls, and faxes. If even a modest fraction of the business migrates to Internet trading systems, Instill could become a giant.

Yet the company must still keep adding value to the transactions, value that goes well beyond just providing a place for up-to-date information and efficient ordering. One way the company has done this by drawing a lesson from the success of Quicken, the popular personal finance program. Quicken users not only enter their transactions into electronic ledgers to pay their bills and balance their checkbooks, but they spend hours massaging the data, creating charts, graphs, budgets and reports, analyzing their past spending, their current investments, and their future options.

Along those lines, Instill developed a set of software, called Advantage, that lets buyers and sellers dive into the data, creating what-if scenarios, generating reports, finding ways to improve efficiencies and lower costs. "The information you can derive from e-commerce is as interesting as the commerce itself," says Andy Cohen, Instill's vice president of marketing. Incidentally, before joining Instill, Cohen helped launch the Quicken.com site while working for Intuit. This value-added approach, he says, will help Instill stave off many hungry new competitors who are following in its path.

Like Instill, the most successful of the new species of cyber-mediaries, or digital middlemen, will be the ones that know their industry cold, the ones that understand not necessarily the bits and bytes of the technology but the particular habits of the business in which they are already a player. Like Instill, if you really want to change an industry, you'll have to dive into the middle and figure out ways to add tremendous value for both the buyer and the seller. In the future, every single type of business, from healthcare, to education, to real estate, to energy, to textiles, will have one or more business-to-business information brokers who do exactly this.

Not Just a Cheap Trade

At first glance, no one would peg Bill Porter as a founder of one of Silicon Valley's hottest Web commerce start-ups. In a culture dominated by the young, the fresh-faced, and the overambitious, Porter is bald, gray, and strikes a grandfatherly profile. But this former navy officer is poised and purposeful as he marches to the podium to give the keynote address for the annual MIT $50K Entrepreneurship Competition, in which student-led teams create business plans and contend for funding. Oddly, Porter begins by plunging into a prolonged and seemingly pointless story, circa 1960, about how he and a small team of engineers developed an electronic switch for diesel locomotives. He's rambling on about rusty old trains to a crowd of entrepreneur-wannabes who came to hear about making money on the Internet. Confused audience members start turning their heads and squinting at one another, and after a while they don't seem to be paying any attention at all.

Finally Porter reveals what purports to be the moral of the tale: "It's the achievement that counts," he declares with a flourish of idealism, "not the money." The students don't quite know what to make of it, until he adds, "Now don't get me wrong, the money is nice too." Applause.

Midway in his career as a physicist and inventor, Porter earned an MBA at MIT's Sloan School and then began applying his scientific insights to the world of business. By 1982 he founded E*Trade Group Inc. with the vision that more and more institutional investment firms would need to move to all-computerized trading systems. He developed his own software and trading network and began as a service bureau, processing transactions electronically for Charles Schwab Corp., Fidelity Investments, and other big-name clients. When he became familiar with what actually goes on among brokers of stocks and bonds—that the profits are shockingly fat and the business is terribly inefficient—Porter naturally began wondering what it would take to change more dramatically the way the industry works.

Some 10 years after founding E*Trade, Porter decided that the time was right to cut directly into the business of his top customers. The year was 1992, when only about 1 million U.S. households were connected to a commercial online service. And E*Trade, based in Silicon Valley, still only had five employees. But by the following year, it began offering online stock trading on CompuServe and America Online. E*Trade wasn't the first to do so. A unit of Donaldson Lufkin & Jenrette (DLJ) had established an online brokerage on Prodigy as early as 1988. (The average number of daily trades that first year was eight!) But by the time the Web came along, E*Trade had become the most aggressive in expanding the market, advertising and marketing itself as the future of finance. ("Someday, we'll all trade this way" was the slogan.) As a result, it was adding 1,000 new customer accounts per day through much of 1996.

And at a time when most Web start-ups were losing money, E*Trade became a rare bird indeed: It was profitable. The company began a string of quarters in which it was posting between 10 and 15 percent net profits at a time when others were nonchalantly ringing up seven-digit losses. Oddly, E*Trade's stock performance wasn't quite as rocketlike as those Web start-ups that were deep in the red, but its initial public offering and follow-on offerings were successful enough to allow the company to move into new digs in Palo Alto while ramping up hiring to more than 600 employees.

Porter had also hired a new CEO, Christos Cotsakos, a former executive with Federal Express and the A.C. Neilsen Company who had survived being machine-gunned in the legs as a young army soldier in Vietnam. Perhaps it was no coincidence that Porter wanted a manager who, like himself, was a veteran of real wars. As most vets will tell you, the trick to winning the war isn't just fighting hard but picking the right battles at the right time.

E*Trade had begun by offering $35 trades, but Porter and Cotsakos decided that cutting the price seven times in a period of 18 months was enough. They did not want to engage in Pyrrhic price skirmishes from which there would emerge no real winners. So they held the line at $14.95 and built up a war chest of $200 million in cash mainly through profits.

Even though Porter was stepping back from day-to-day management, he remained chairman emeritus of the company and continued to define its corporate DNA. Most significantly, he was quietly preparing for a shakeout in this new industry. Dozens of fierce competitors had cropped up, from start-ups to some of the world's biggest brokerage houses. Rival Datek slashed its lowest commission to $9.99. Ameritrade plunged to $8, and Suretrade sank to $7.95. What happens when the bear market returns, growth slows, and Darwinian forces put the pressure on companies with no profits? "One day, the market will drop," Porter says, "and we will use that [war chest] money to acquire our rivals."

E*Trade's overall strategy for becoming the long-term survivor in what's shaping up to be a brutal market was this: In the end, it won't matter much whether investors are paying $5 per trade or $25. Eventually, all online brokerages will have prices in that range, and all are far cheaper than full-service brokers and financial advisors who are still charging $300 to $1,000 or more to trade, say, 1,000 shares of Intel. "Price is what hooks them," says Kathy Levinson, president of E*Trade's main business unit. "But this is about more than the cheap trade. It's the customization, the research tools, the portfolio management services, the comfort factor, and the quality of information that makes them stick around."

Instead of a low-cost approach, E*Trade was pursuing a *value-added* approach that applies not only to the online brokerage business but nearly all business that can be conducted over the Web. When buyers and sellers meet, they very much prefer to do so on neutral territory, not on the website of the buyer or the seller itself. But simply executing a trade order on time isn't nearly enough. The transaction must be surrounded with mountains of well-organized information and oceans of easy-to-use services that make customers want to return to this middle ground, this intermediate place, again and again. For instance, E*Trade was among the first online brokerages to offer free analyst reports as well as mortgage and insurance centers. In addition, it stages live chats with top CEOs and institutional investors, plus it maintains an online "water cooler," a bulletin board area where investors go to gab about stocks.

The value-added strategy seemed to be working. E*Trade became the top online-only broker, with market share trailing only that of Schwab, a far larger, older, and well-capitalized company that used its brand clout and its numerous sales offices in every city to muscle into the new market. Yet it seemed that the market was plenty big enough for both of them, as the number of online traders was expected to quadruple within a short time, from 4 million customer accounts in 1997 to more than 16 million by 2002.

Higher Stakes

Everything was moving along rather steadily until E*Trade was forced to adapt to sudden changes in the marketplace. Competitors were proliferating to a point where it was clear that being a leader in this business was going to be more expensive than previously thought. First, to prevent system crashes on high-volume trading days, like the one it had experienced one frantic day in October 1997, E*Trade rushed to overhaul its back-order processing systems, at a cost of $75 million. That effort paid off. In September 1998, when the Dow once again dropped more than 500 points and single-day volume almost broke the previous record, E*Trade's systems handled the load almost flawlessly.

Most of its competitors fared well too. The new industry had surpassed a major hurdle. Online investing was becoming mainstream, as it was already accounting for more than 25 percent of combined retail trading volume on the NASDAQ and New York Stock Exchange, up from a small fraction of 1 percent just a few years earlier.

By now there were more than 80 online brokers competing with it, and E*Trade was learning something valuable about customer behavior: There was a powerful lock-in effect. People who put their assets into one online brokerage service tended to stay put for a long time. More than 95 percent of customers who had opened E*Trade accounts stuck with the service, says Levinson. That meant only one thing: In this period of rapid growth, the dominant players of the future had to acquire as many loyal customers as they could as soon as possible. If this was indeed the case, E*Trade would have to begin digging into Porter's arsenal of cash, which had recently been augmented by a $400 million equity investment from Japan's Softbank, a high-tech investment firm that also owned a large chunk of Yahoo.

The result was "Destination E*Trade." In a relentless, $150 million mass-media advertising blitz, E*Trade fought to position itself as a daily gathering spot for all investors. It greatly expanded the information and services that were available for free to any visitor, not just those with accounts. Anyone, for instance, could now go there to obtain live stock quotes or call up graphs comparing the performance among 4,000 different mutual funds at no cost. At the same time, it spent heavily to develop custom editions for European and Asian investors. E*Trade felt it really had no choice in the matter. If it didn't do these things, the company reasoned, others would.

Porter's conservative plan was gone and, as a result, the business model went haywire. Because of the heavy advertising, E*Trade was now spending more than $300 to acquire each new customer. By contrast, Ameritrade was spending $91 and Schwab was spending about $79. They were all too high, but E*Trade was on the highest wire of all. If an online broker has a customer acquisition cost of around $40, it might have a chance of making back that money in profits within a year or so. But when it's more than $300, it could take as long as five years. And in this business, when you try to peer that far into the future, your vision gets obscured by dense fog and thick smoke.

Cotsakos was forced to break the bad news to Wall Street: These costly initiatives would wipe out all profits for at least a year, perhaps two. The company was heading into the unknown. Would it meet its goal of garnering millions of new online accounts and emerge as a Goliath of the online financial services world? Or would the cost of acquiring each new customer be too much for the firm to sustain? Although its stock began rising, buoyed by the perverse logic of Internet investors, E*Trade seemed to be weakening itself financially at a critical time, when the real giants of the industry were finally beginning to make their moves. Persevering through the next phase of evolution would require winning a game with much higher stakes than anyone had imagined.

Here Come the Giants

For a while, many of those really big players were not only the laggards in the race to become financial cybermediaries, but some were actually fighting the trend rather vigorously.

Merrill Lynch & Co. vice chairman John "Launny" Steffens, for one, began conducting a very public campaign to convince investors that Internet stock trading was bad for them. "The do-it-yourself model of investing, centered on Internet trading, should be regarded as a serious threat to Americans' financial lives," Steffens declared at a PC Expo conference in New York. "This approach to financial decision-making doesn't serve clients well, and it's a business model that won't deliver lasting value."

Steffens cited a study showing that online investors place four times as many trades as their offline counterparts. And he compared such high-volume trading to out-and-out gambling. "It's like going to Las Vegas and betting on black or red," he said.

As the person who commands Merrill's army of 15,000 stock brokers—one of the world's largest corporate sales forces—Steffens obviously has a vested interest in protecting the high commissions they charge. But his public battle was perplexing because it seemed so hopeless: A certain segment of investors adamantly preferred online trading, and this market was only going to grow larger. And it's the brokers themselves who shoulder most of the risk here: Their base salary is typically a pittance, as they rely on commissions for a living. But for the time being, at least, Merrill can take comfort that its account base of more than 9 million clients is larger than that of all the online brokers combined. If Steffens managed somehow to hold on to that lucrative franchise long enough, it would at least buy Merrill more time to consider what to do about this inevitable encroachment.

With time on its side, Merrill plodded onto the Web. Its first step was to roll out an online brokerage of its own. But rather than offering Internet trading to the general public, it provided it as an option only for current clients. Instead of low-cost trades, commissions would still range in the hundreds of dollars for typical transactions. The plan seemed so nonsensical that it bordered on the insulting. But it was only the beginning.

Merrill then began to offer its equity research for free to the public during a four-month trial period. These research reports were crown-jewel assets to the company, previously available only to its well-heeled individual and institutional investors. The plan was to show potential clients that Merrill's value-added information, combined with the guidance of a live human broker, was superior and much more profitable than doing it yourself on the Web. Nevertheless, Steffens denied that he was doing this to fend off competition from online brokers. "They can put whatever spin they want on it," countered E*Trade's Cotsakos, "but they had to do it because of the success of online investing."

Then, to reduce its bloated cost structure—the extravagant expenses and fully staffed workforce that it had built up over the years—Merrill swung the ax, laying off 3,400 employees, about 5 percent of its workforce. As it became leaner and meaner and more aggressive on the Internet, Merrill, like it or not, was becoming more like E*Trade and the other online brokers every day. At the same time, though, E*Trade was adding more and more value and content, thus becoming more and more like Merrill. The two styles of trading were still miles apart, but they were coevolving and adapting to each other's environments. One could envision the eventual day when they would meet somewhere in the middle.

Online brokerage accounts are not just about stock trading anymore. Many of these upstarts are offering check-writing, bill payment, home mortgage shopping, life insurance, retirement accounts, and credit cards—the services that have traditionally been the domain of banks. Online brokerages are well on their way toward becoming the one-stop financial megamarkets that today's superbanks say they want to be. Consumers and institutional clients want access to a complete range of financial products and services. Yes, the traditional providers of these services are merging and forming alliances so that an entire menu can be presented in one place. But the race to create the ultimate financial superstores will be won by the companies that add the most value to online transactions.

This sets up a showdown not only between the Web brokers and the Merrill Lynches of the world but also between the Web brokers and the nationwide banking conglomerates that have emerged from the frenzy of consolidation in the industry. Banks, of course, are used to market erosion. In 1977 banks held 25 percent of financial assets of U.S. households, but that dropped to 12 percent by 1997, says the management consulting firm Ernst & Young. Over the same period, the share held by asset managers, including brokers and mutual fund companies, rose from 37 percent to 67 percent. Still, banks aren't exactly comfortable with this fate.

Their problem is that the number of online banking accounts have been growing much more slowly than online brokerage accounts. Gomez Advisors, of Concord, Massachusetts, estimates that only about 2 million people were doing online banking by 1998. As the first bank with 1 million online customers, Wells Fargo has been in the lead. But if Wells Fargo, Citigroup, First Union, and all the other megabanks don't adapt faster, many analysts believe that upstart online brokerages will control more than half of the projected $700 billion of assets in online accounts by 2002.

In the future, most financial giants will be forced to straddle both worlds. Fleet Financial Group, for instance, is one of the largest megabanks but also owns the online Quick & Reilly brokerage and Suretrade.com. Meanwhile, Morgan Stanley Dean Witter & Co. has been holding onto its legion of human brokers at the same time that it has been heavily promoting Discover Brokerage Direct, its public Web service. Old-timer DLJ has been doing much the same with its DLJdirect service. And mutual fund kingpin Fidelity has quickly become one of the top-five online brokers in terms of market share.

As these giants discover the lower costs and high customer retention rates that are possible through cybermediation, we can expect more of these cross-channel matchups. For this reason, E*Trade itself may very well be vulnerable to a takeover by a financial colossus that it now considers the enemy.

The leaders of the industry are bracing for the next wave of technology-driven consolidation and a Darwinian shakeout. "Finance is a pure information processing game," says David E. Shaw, CEO of D.E. Shaw & Co., Inc., the super–high-tech hedge fund where Amazon.com's Jeff Bezos used to work. "A lot of people in the business are doing things that should be done by computers," Shaw concludes. "Our industry will shrink and it should shrink."

Ultimately, everyone will realize that many of the *labor-mediated* services that financial firms had offered in the past are now morphing into *technology-mediated* services. And there is big money in cybermediation. The firms that add the most new value to a wide range of financial chores will be the profit leaders of the future. Several big winners will appear. And at the same time, the consolidating financial services environment simply won't continue to give life to the companies that fail to use technology aggressively.

Home Improvement

Let's turn to a different type of cybermediation. Whereas financial markets are global in scope, this other market is intensely local. Whereas finance is consolidating rapidly around a few well-known brand names, this other one is highly fragmented, with brands that aren't very prominent at all. Instead of a business that is almost totally driven by information and data that can be presented and massaged on computers, this one requires people to get dirt under their fingernails.

Welcome to the nightmarish netherworld of home improvement, in which finding the right products can be an endless source of frustration and in which finding a quality contractor who returns your phone calls can be an exercise in futility. Home improvement projects can devour one's time and sap one's creative energy. That's why a whole new breed of home improvement cybermediaries are cropping up to attack the needs of people who are renovating kitchens, bathrooms, basements, or entire houses. But overall, this is an underexploited area, as there are few, if any, dominant project-oriented brands on the Web.

The opportunity is enormous. Estimated at $200 billion annually in the United States, this market comprises more than 1 million companies and contractors. The Home Depot and other superstores may own a good portion of the market's lower end, but then there are tens of thousands of local hardware, lumber, and paint stores providing access to basic materials. And don't forget the endless Yellow Page listings of local contractors, many of whom are unreliable or worse. Plus, there are thousands of high-end product showrooms all over the country that cater to more upscale clients. In short, the market is ripe for a cybermediary to find a way to match confused and frustrated buyers with the right sellers and contractors.

One start-up that has honed in on cybermediating the home improvement market is a Boston-based company called Home-Portfolio.com. It aims to pull everything together for high-end consumers. In essence, the site serves as a replacement for those manila folders—packed with information, contractor names, and estimates—that people renovating their homes clutch like security blankets. These manila folders typically are filled with scraps of paper with phone numbers and product specs, ads torn from magazines, notes from phone conversations, price sheets, brochures, and all kinds of other fruits of laborious research. Tom Ashbrook, HomePortfolio's CEO and a former ad salesman with the *Boston Globe,* predicts that if one website can organize all that research, information, and purchasing, consumers will flock to it and use it as their primary project management tool.

As evidence that people are intensely interested in this category of information, Ashbrook points to that fact that Americans buy 25 million issues of home design and home improvement magazines each year. Many of the ads and layouts in the glossiest of these magazines feature such expensive and aspirational designs that Ashbrook refers to it as "wealth porn."

The HomePortfolio site is organized around your own "Personal Portfolio," an online folder that saves the product information and online brochures that you choose. You can search the site according to the room that you're renovating, with sublistings that focus on different products that go in the room. For instance, in the kitchen section, there is a research area for countertops, refrigerators, stoves, and flooring. Each area includes information on product brands—including prices, pictures, video snippets, specifications, ideas, and e-mail addresses. Some of these home remodeling and appliance brands may very well dominate their respective categories, but the neophyte home renovator is often unfamiliar with them.

The company aims to make most of its money by selling sponsorships in these portfolio areas. The site tries to list information on every brand, but those that pay a fee go to the top of the list or get displayed prominently on one side of the screen. In the early stages of starting the company, Ashbrook encountered fierce resistance from his potential sponsors, because side-by-side listings could enable consumers to do easy price comparisons and shop based only on that criterion. "There is this assumption that the Net commoditizes purchasing," says Ashbrook, "and it scares the hell out of the manufacturers. But this isn't about discounting. This is about high, white-glove service."

In most cases, consumers won't be purchasing high-end products such as granite countertops and chrome stoves online. Rather they would do their research here, then visit a local showroom. The site offers an easy way to book those appointments, which leads to another source of revenue: commissions from customer referrals.

Yet HomePortfolio initially failed on one important count: The site offered little more than a convenient way to sift through and organize glossy photos and electronic brochures. Indeed, the service was far more useful to the *sellers,* the product companies, than it was to the *buyers.* The makers of kitchen countertops and flooring get to reach a highly interested base of consumers, but pleasing them is only half of what makes for successful cybermediation. For customers, finding the perfect appliances and cabinets and such is the easiest part. The hard part is finding somebody who will install everything properly, on time, at a reasonable price. For a cybermediary to bring true value to the transaction, it needs to see the customer through the entire process.

Handyman Helper

A rival service called ImproveNet has taken a crack at this, actually going to the trouble of evaluating more than 600,000 contractors nationwide. Founded in 1996 by a couple of entrepreneurs with experience in real estate, business, and software, the Redwood City, California, company has assembled a database of contractors, architects, and designers from all over the country. The goal is to make it easy for consumers to find honest and able people to do the job and do it right.

Everyone has heard of horror stories about sloppy house painters or about the kitchen renovation from hell. "It's complex and daunting to pick out what goes into that kitchen," says Robert Stevens, ImproveNet's founder and president. He jokes that his website should also refer customers to good divorce lawyers. Home improvement projects, especially kitchens and bathrooms, are usually initiated by the wife and end up costing an average 60 percent more than she told her husband they would, he says.

Before being listed in ImproveNet's database, each contractor must submit to a series of screening tests. ImproveNet checks credit reports, any history of consumer complaints or legal judgments, as well as insurance and license status. About 25 percent are rejected because they don't pass the screening test, and 15 percent are rejected because they fail to disclose enough information. Contractors do not have to pay anything for the screening.

This information is hard to assemble, which is what gives ImproveNet such great potential value. Anyone getting into the business of becoming a cybermediary in any industry could benefit from this simple rule: The more difficult it is to obtain a certain set of information, the greater the competitive edge it can give you in the marketplace. Like HomePortfolio, almost anyone can assemble a set of electronic brochures, but there may very well be only a few places to tap into an extensive database of prescreened contractors.

Here's how ImproveNet works: The customer enters extensive project information, including size of the rooms in need of renovation, what exactly needs to be done, what new material or appliances are needed, an estimated budget, a time frame, along with typical name, address, and contact data. ImproveNet faxes the project information—but not the customer's name or address—to about 40 to 50 contractors in the customer's local region. Why send so many long-distance faxes and not just e-mail it? "Because contractors are the lowest of the low tech," Stevens says. Many do not have computers yet.

Typically, only three or four of those contracts will respond to the fax. The others might not be available for the requested time period, or they might not be equipped to do that specific job. Those three or four contractors must pay $6 to go on the "Recommended" list, which then is e-mailed to the customer. Both contractors and customer are then instructed to call one another right away. If the customer does indeed sign up with someone on the short list, ImproveNet collects a "win fee" from the contractor—usually $100 to $150, or about 1 percent of the estimated cost of the average project. The customer, meanwhile, doesn't have to pay ImproveNet anything. (Stevens says that contractors are instructed not to pass along that 1 percent fee to customers by jacking up their price.)

Since I was planning a total gut job and renovation of my own kitchen, I decided to see if ImproveNet could help. Within three days of sending in my project details over the Web, I received an e-mail list of four contractors. I was told that all had clean, upstanding records and all were eagerly awaiting my business.

Still, I felt a strong need for even more information. After all, whoever my wife and I pick will pretty much be spending a month in our home. Are there any personal recommendations on file? Do they specialize in any particular kind of work? Do they have experience with my kind of kitchen? To me, they were just names on a list. Stevens admits that this is a shortcoming that the company is working on. Ideally, he says, there should be a comprehensive file of information about each contractor, including references and comments from past customers. That information will take some time to gather.

Three of the contractors on my list were prompt enough to call right away, and my wife and I scheduled an appointment with one to come over. But since this contractor had a showroom in a nearby town, we decided to pay an impromptu visit beforehand. We wanted to touch the countertops and open and close cabinets, not just see brochures. So we packed up the kids and drove over there.

The experience was rather strange. First off, the showroom was no longer on the main street, as its address indicated. When we finally found the entrance and walked inside, the owner, a laidback, 60ish man named John, explained that he no longer needs expensive, storefront real estate. He cut his floorspace in half and just kept the back room. With more and more referrals coming in over the Internet, he figures, who needs physical space? All the cabinets and appliances are delivered direct from the factories anyhow.

The fact that the showroom was unimpressive didn't really matter to us much. After all, even the biggest and most lavish ones can keep only a small fraction of product on hand. What did matter was his approach. He kept steering us to the cheapest materials and the cheapest options available. Later, after visiting our kitchen, the design he wanted to create for us was based on the wrong assumption that, like most of his clients, we don't do much cooking. "I usually put the oven in the corner because it's the least used appliance," he said. Yes, he was prompt and professional. And in the end, he came up with a reasonable bid and design plan. But, overall, it was a giant mismatch. He just wasn't the right contractor for us. We ended up going with a kitchen designer and a contractor who came highly recommended by close friends who had recently completed similar projects.

And this is where ImproveNet fell short: It is able to match buyers with local sellers who are willing and able to do a project. But is it a high-quality match? Are those sellers right for this buyer with this particular project, taste, and expectation? ImproveNet's Stevens agrees that this a problem. These types of personal recommendations from people with experience are hard to simulate on the Web. But he also agrees that he must try. Perhaps the ultimate goal is some sort of "collaborative filtering," in which software matches you with a contractor who completed a similar project nearby, one that was completed on time and in which the customer was satisfied with the work.

Despite the imperfections of its initial service, ImproveNet may be sitting on buried treasure. No one else seems to have assembled the database it now maintains. In its first full year online, ImproveNet fulfilled requests for more than 20,000 projects, representing $1.4 billion in spending, according to Stevens. The company has raised $22 million from a group of venture capitalists and Allstate Insurance. (Allstate is heavily involved in this market because damage, disasters, and accidents are a leading cause of home improvement.)

In the future, ImproveNet could become the cybermediary to beat in the home improvement industry. Stevens wants to expand the service so that it becomes the central spot not only for obtaining contractors, designers, and other professionals but also for researching product information, buying appliances, and getting home insurance and home equity loans. "This is one of those dark ages industries," he says. "It's large, fragmented and inefficient, yet people have the same universal questions, problems, and concerns."

Of course, the market is so huge that the 800-pound gorillas of the business might smell the same opportunity. With 118,000 employees, The Home Depot is already in the business of helping customers hire contractors to install the products purchased at its stores. Yet its initial website was rather unsophisticated and didn't even hint at entering ImproveNet's territory. "We at The Home Depot understand that there is a great demand for our products to be available on-line for the purposes of viewing, searching and yes, purchasing," explains a notice at its site. "Be assured that we are researching all such Internet opportunities. Before launching a program of such magnitude, we need to make sure it will not prohibit us from our ultimate goal of providing you, our customer, with the best customer service possible."

They're right, sort of. For The Home Depot, there probably is some business to be had selling its 50,000 in-stock items over the Web. No one necessarily wants to buy home improvement products directly from the manufacturer. If an intermediary can add value, then all the better, but it has to be an enormous amount of value. In this case, the digital middleman has to be willing to get his hands dirty, at least metaphorically. That's why the real opportunity here goes way beyond shopping. It's about becoming the company that recommends the right people, about evolving into the company that can make sure the job gets done.

EXECUTIVE SURVIVAL GUIDE:
CYBERMEDIATION

▶ If you're a middleman—a go-between for buyers and sellers—recognize that the Internet is bringing about big changes in your market. You must actively accelerate those changes before they engulf you.

▶ To take advantage of this opportunity before your rivals do, you must develop a neutral online meeting space where buyers and sellers can find one another and place and receive orders efficiently.

▶ But performing the transactions online, at a lower cost, isn't nearly enough. You must add tremendous value, inventing new interactive features and services that smooth out the process and lead to a new surge in buying and selling.

▶ If you do not aim to become a cybermediary yourself, consider alternative strategies: Lessen your dependence on processing commodity transactions (i.e., airline reservations, stock trades), then focus on the human touch, beefing up personal service, professional expertise, and consulting that a website can't match.

▶ Or you can affiliate with a cybermediary to generate sales leads, as traditional Realtors and car dealers are now doing.

▶ If all else fails, get out of the way and find something else to do, because your business may not be here in a few years. Benefit soon from rapidly consolidating markets and sell your company before it's too late.

INTEGRATE DIGITAL COMMERCE
WITH ABSOLUTELY EVERYTHING

Developing Real-World Integration

There's something curious going on at the REI store nearest you. A wilderness, camping, and outdoors retailer that started in Seattle about 60 years ago, Recreational Equipment Inc. in recent years has been installing banks of computer kiosks displaying its online catalog in all of its 50-plus locations.

Why would REI do this? The largest of its stores are such entertaining, event-driven places to be and be seen that customers refer to it as "Hike Town." The company's flagship location in Seattle is a 100,000-square-foot, $28-million, two-story wilderness mecca. It not only features the expected assortment of sleeping bags, tents, hiking gear, and portable stoves but also boasts a rain-forest room for testing harsh-weather gear, a climbing structure for practicing footing technique, a cooking lab for trying out culinary equipment, a mountain bike track, and a 100-seat café for pure, down-home socializing. Isn't there enough to do here already? Why on Earth would anyone need to shop via a website catalog while in a store like this?

Actually, there are at least three reasons: First, much of the merchandise isn't always in stock, especially at some of the smaller REI outlets. With self-service computers in the store, shoppers can hop online, choose from a wider range of goods—more than 10,000 items in all—buy what they want with their credit card, and have it delivered to their home or for pickup at the store. This allows the stores to add "virtual inventory" beyond what customers can see in front of them.

"People don't go into the store to play on the computers," says Matt Hyde, REI's director of online sales. "But if you're in the Wisconsin store and you're getting ready to go climbing in Yosemite, and you need our haul bag, and that store doesn't carry it, we'll ship it to you for an extra $2.50."

Second, the website is stockpiled with deep data on each product. These are the detailed specifications that hardcore campers and hikers can't get enough of and store employees can't possibly memorize. So, if a patron wants to see a chart comparing the density—the weight relative to size—of 30 different sleeping bags, she can refer to the website, generate a chart, and print it.

Finally, the third reason to have computers in the store is so customers can do things that stores of this type don't normally offer. For instance, customers can print out customized, full-color, high-resolution, topographic HorizonMaps of almost any wilderness destination on Earth. Or they can log onto REI Adventures, an online travel agency that provides information and bookings for hundreds of adventure trips. With all these options, it's no wonder that a typical store visit lasts nearly two hours.

There's also a bonus benefit of having customers surf your website while they are standing in your physical location. This way, when they get home, the customers are already trained; they now know their way around your site, and they are much more likely to remember to visit the site again and again. When you look at it this way, an old-fashioned, brick-and-mortar building can become the best advertisement any Web business can buy.

But here's the killer part, the part that crystallizes the connection between the physical and digital worlds. REI's website not only lists the locations of each store but always promotes a current roster of local events. If there is a bicycle maintenance clinic happening in the Cary, North Carolina, store or a talk by a park ranger about "living with predators" at the Fort Collins, Colorado, store or if the Redmond, Washington, store is organizing a series of hikes up Mount Rainier, the website will tell you that you simply must go. This, of course, drives people back to the store again, and perhaps even gets them socializing with other people who also like shopping there.

The REI catalog is integrated in a similar way. In addition to picturing its products on full-color glossy pages, the 10-million copies of the catalog that REI mails each year encourage customers to visit the website for more detailed product information and a wider selection. The Web address is promoted on the front cover and on almost every page-fold. Then, at the website, the home page includes a blurb that says: "Order our new catalog!" REI constantly has its customers looping back and forth and back again and again among all of its three main retail channels.

The latest destination on this grand loop is the newer REI-Outlet.com site, which skimps on all the bells and whistles of the regular site and simply offers "off-price" or "closeout" bargains. Visitors can sign up for the BargainSleuth e-mail notification service, which alerts customers when a requested item goes on sale. The discount outlet site, of course, links back to the regular REI site as well.

The company's total investment in its Web presence has been considerable. REI has spent at least $1 million developing the site and integrating it with all of its legacy information systems at its headquarters. "And we think we've been frugal," Hyde says.

But the return has been even greater. From the initial planning stages in 1995, REI's Web venture was treated as a "a profit center rather than a marketing expense," Hyde says, "which was highly unusual at the time." The site brought in about $10 million in sales in its first year online, triple what the company expected. That's equivalent to one of REI's larger physical stores. Naturally, the Web has broadened REI's presence globally too. With translated versions in French, German, Spanish, and Japanese, REI is now selling in 40 countries.

Most important, it has reinforced the loyalty of its customers. How loyal are they? Here's a clue: They are so committed to REI that more than a million of them have paid $15 for a lifetime membership card. Since REI is run as a customer cooperative, membership confers actual ownership of the company. The owners elect the board of directors and are entitled to a patronage dividend at the end of every year, a rebate based on a percentage of how much they've spent. The percentage ranges from 5 to 10 percent or more, depending on how profitable the company is. Based on its 1998 sales of $587 million, for instance, the company declared a total patronage refund of $31 million to more than 5 million members. These numbers make REI the largest consumer cooperative in America.

To some businesspeople, it might sound a bit anticapitalist to go so far as to give the majority of your profits back to your customers. But REI's employees still get paid, the executives are still compensated, and management still has control over how much it wants to invest on expansion and future business development. The customers simply get what's left over at the end of all that. And knowing that fact causes the customers to spend more. They are simply more inclined to visit an REI store, shop the REI catalog, or order via the rei.com whenever they are in the market for outdoor gear.

This focus on the customer is what drove REI to become one of the first companies to accomplish meaningful real-world integration among all modern channels of distribution. "Many businesses have been like deer frozen in the headlights because of their channel conflicts," Hyde says. "They see the Web as competing with their other lines of business. But we take Web orders from the core Seattle customers who drive by our stores every day. Many customers are multichannel customers. We can't choose how our customers want to shop. So we offer any product, any time, any place, and answer any question."

Indeed, every company, Web-based or otherwise, should try this interesting discipline: Act as if your company is, in effect, owned by your customers—not by self-interested venture capitalists, not by shareholders who might hold your stock for only a few hours at a time, not even by employees. At bottom, real-world integration is a survival strategy that should be aimed at retaining those customers for life.

Revenge of the Little Guy

You cannot log onto the Internet from a CompUSA store. Let's think about this for a moment. With 200 locations, CompUSA is the country's largest chain of high-tech megastores. Each store is stocked with rows upon rows of PCs and thousands upon thousands of pieces of merchandise with website addresses printed on them. If a certain hotselling PC is out of stock at a specific location but available for purchase at compusa.com, why not allow the customer to log onto the Net, purchase the machine online and have it shipped to their home or office? "Sorry," says a young salesman at CompUSA's Boston location, "but we can only get onto our internal company network from the store." But there are, like, millions of computers here, and all of them come with Web browsers pre-loaded on the hard drive! The salesman shrugs and throws up his hands.

That's only the beginning. You would think that customers

shopping at barnesandnoble.com would at least be able to order a book online, then choose to pick it up at one of the stores near where they live or work. This way, they could save shipping charges and perhaps get the book faster. No dice. What if you purchased a book at the website but didn't like it and wanted to exchange it at a store for something else? Believe it or not, the stores literally would not accept it. Here's another glitch: Say you are in one of Barnes & Noble's 1,000 stores and you wanted to find a book but couldn't quite remember the title or the author's name. Why not just hop on a nearby computer and search the company's Web catalog? Sorry, the store computers are for use by employees only. Company policy.

"Our website is really run as a separate company, and we plan to keep it that way," says a barnesandnoble.com customer service representative. "There are benefits to keeping them separate," he adds. "For instance, we don't have to charge sales taxes." That's because the laws governing mail-order sales require taxing only the patrons who live in a state where you have a physical presence. (Since barnesandnoble.com is operated out of New York, customers in the other 49 states shop tax-free.)

Needless to say, billionaire Jeff Bezos is delighted about all of this. When pressed, the Amazon.com founder and CEO will admit that he is actually fearful that Barnes & Noble will eventually reverse these silly policies, implement these services, and do a whole lot more. "Physical retailers can set up effective feedback loops between stores and websites," Bezos says flatly. Of course, this knowledge is of little use to him. After all, integrating the Web with the real world is just about the *only* strategy that Amazon.com cannot implement. So why is it that *he* knows this, whereas most big retailers act as if they don't?

If Amazon.com can't do it—at least not yet—and Barnes & Noble won't do it, who will? Amazingly, the first booksellers to attempt real-world integration have been the little guys, the independent shops that were supposed to have been pulverized—first by the megachains and then by the Web. It's sad but true that hundreds of small bookstores have indeed been shutting their lights for good in recent years. Independent booksellers now only hold onto about 15 percent of the market, down from 33 percent in 1991, according to the American Booksellers Association. Many small bookshop owners—some 300 in 1997 alone—have already gone down with the ship.

Yet some are using technology as a weapon to strike back. Brookline Booksmith, located just outside of Boston, is a case in point. In 1994, when a big Barnes & Noble opened just a couple blocks away, the store was in immediate danger of going under after nearly 35 years as the only general-interest bookstore in a town of 55,000 people. Adding injury to insult, the rival store opened at the same time the Booksmith's landlord quadrupled the rent. Things got pretty grim. "We had an employee meeting, and we all left wanting to cry," says store manager and co-owner Dana Brigham.

But the store's employees decided to enact a policy of "tenacious defiance," which involved "reinventing and relearning why we were here in the first place," Brigham says. "I'd be damned if they were going to hurt us." The store indeed lost money for the next four years in a row. But by 1998, the Booksmith was once again profitable. And its tenacity was rewarded with a rather high compliment: The editors of *Publishers Weekly* named it America's "bookseller of the year."

The Web played a key role in the comeback effort. In late 1996 a 25-year-old store employee named Kip Jacobson started developing a website after-hours on his home computer. "It could just as easily not have happened at all," Jacobson says. Only months after it was up and running did it start being taken seriously by his boss and coworkers. Brigham cleared away an area for Jacobson to work in the store's back room and dubbed him the full-time Webmaster.

Brigham began noticing that the site was fortifying the store's business in a number of ways. Chief among them has been as a way to get more people in for events. Within a few months, about 1,000 people who had visited the site signed up for the monthly e-mail newsletter. The newsletter informs patrons of author signings, readings, parties, new releases, special discounts, and events such as "bring your bookclub night."

When author Barbara Kingsolver was first scheduled to appear at the store, those who visited the website and received the e-mail newsletter heard about it before employees had a chance to put up the traditional paper flyers at the store entrance. Before they knew it, 600 people bought tickets to the reading, which had to be held across the street in a movie theater. Nearly half of those attendees bought Kingsolver's new novel.

For one unique party on a fall Friday evening, called "Local Authors Night," the store recruited 20 authors from all over Massachusetts to run the place—work the registers, stock the shelves, and chat with customers about books over food and drinks. Thanks in part to great word-of-Web, the place was jammed, and the store did 50 percent more than its typical business.

Brigham eventually embarked on a strategy of integrating the Web into everything that the store does, placing Jacobson in charge of all the store's marketing efforts. Signs in the store now promote the many different uses of the website. And visitors to the site can do things such as set up a book-referral appointment with one of the store's employees. The idea began as a gift recommendation service during Christmas season. The customer describes the books that friends or relatives have most enjoyed and the bookseller will point to other titles that they will probably like. It's similar to Amazon's personal recommendation service except that it's done by a real live human bookworm rather than a computer program.

All physical retail stores—indeed all businesses—have to

evolve into more complex, hybrid species, integrating their Web presence with everything else they do. No longer should the Web economy exist in some parallel cyberuniverse. For booksellers, the vision is rather straightforward: They must use all means necessary to promote the news, searching, and ordering features of their websites *while customers are browsing in the store,* even if it's as simple as giving out bookmarks with the URL printed on them. At the same time, their websites must promote events and community functions happening at the stores itself.

That's what Amazon.com's Bezos means by an effective feedback loop. Physical and digital must reinforce one another and compensate for each other's weaknesses. The store drives traffic to the site and the site drives traffic to the store.

Yet much more needs to be done in this realm. Everyone in retail knows that a large percentage of people who come into a store leave without buying anything. Maybe they're browsing and didn't see something that caught their eye, or maybe they're looking for something they couldn't find. In bookstores, you could walk up front and ask the clerk, "Do you have this title? Is it coming in?" and the clerk will type into a terminal and peer in a database and reply, "We don't have it but we can get it for you in a week or so." Yet many people are too shy to ask, or feel the clerks seem too busy, or figure they'll just get it on the Web.

To attack this problem, imagine if a bookstore replaced an entire aisle of books with a row of computers. Not to create a cybercafé, but just for the purpose of displaying only that store's website and online catalog for customer use, as at REI. It's likely that the row of computers would keep people in the store longer, make them more likely to buy something, and thus be more profitable per square foot than the original row of merchandise. Customers could create a personal account, then reserve an item they see for later pickup.

Then, when they're on the Web at home weeks later and want

to go to an online retailer, they're more likely to return to the site from the local store, the one they already know how to use. The bottom line is that current customers probably will purchase a much higher percentage of their products from that local store.

The Missing Link

The membership card in the REI story serves as a harbinger of things to come. More and more companies should be taking customer relationships to the next level by issuing club cards—either paid or free of charge—and then giving customers many different reasons for using them. No one wants a wallet bulging with dozens of such cards, but that's okay, because now it is possible for a single card to manage dozens of complex relationships with ease.

What kind of card can do this? Why, a smart card, of course. A smart card is a credit card–size device with a built-in microprocessor and computer memory that can act as the bridge between the Web world and the physical world. Indeed, it can be the missing link that finally connects two previously separate forms of commerce.

Stop laughing. We all know that in many parts of the world, particularly in a certain country just south of Canada, the smart card has been a spectacular failure and the whipping boy of the banking and retail industry. That's because smart cards have been used in exceedingly dumb ways. In the United States, smart cards have unfortunately become synonymous with stored-value cards, as a replacement for petty, carry-around cash. Unlike a credit card or a debit card, which simply authorizes you to perform transactions, a stored-value card has a chip that contains codes representing money itself, to be replenished at an ATM. Merchants don't have to contact anyone; they only have to swipe the card through a reader to take the money from you. If you lose the card, you lose the money.

High-profile tests of these kind of cards were conducted at the Olympic Village in Atlanta in 1996 and on the Upper West Side of Manhattan in 1998. Both were flops. Bills and coins are a tough opponent. People like to use real money for small purchases, perhaps for deeply embedded psychological reasons. Consumers are comfortable with cash. And there is little demand for banishing coins and greenbacks from everyday life. As a result, the stored-value function of smart cards is simply a solution to a problem that doesn't really exist.

The reason why smart cards have already caught on in Europe, however, has little to do with replacing money as we know it and much to do with the nature of continent's telephone systems. Because of their history as entrenched government monopolies, the phone systems of many European nations are quite expensive to use, even for local calls. This has produced a widespread demand for free calls, better known as fraud. When given the chance, young hooligans will kick open the coin boxes of pay phones, and older hooligans will steal calling card numbers.

Smart cards with complex security chips and a prestored amount of calling credits can eradicate both types of crime. At about $2 a pop to issue, they are well worth it to European phone companies that have experienced much higher levels of fraud, on average, per account. In the United States, phone fraud is still a problem, but it generally factors out to less than $2 per subscriber. Thus, issuing the smart card just to wipe out fraud hasn't been worth it from the point of view of U.S. phone companies. Indeed, a U.S. phone company will connect a calling card call without authenticating who you are. If fraud happens, it tries to tackle the problem after the fact.

This, of course, is already changing with the great proliferation of cellular phones and personal digital communications (PCS) devices. These types of phones are much more expensive to use than traditional land-based ones. Naturally, greater fraud rates follow, as criminals scan the airwaves picking out code numbers transmitted by cell phones. As a result, many new digital PCS phones are controlled by a credit card–size device that not only authenticates who you are and manages your account but contains a microprocessor powerful enough and memory large enough to run simple, computerlike applications, such as storing address books and receiving e-mail. If you slip the card out of your phone and into your friend's phone, your friend's phone simply works exactly as if it were yours. Just enter in your password and dial away.

These are smart cards. And believe it or not, tens of millions of people already have them and use them without thinking much about them. Smart cards are so much more capable than standard-issue magnetic strip cards that they are actually turning into computers in and of themselves. While a smart card doesn't have its own input and output devices, it can be slipped into a computer and programmed.

And as such, these card-based computers are subject to Moore's Law. The famously clairvoyant prognostication of Intel Corp. cofounder Gordon Moore states that the potential power of microprocessors will double every 18 months. While that has indeed been true in the computing world for some 30 years, smart cards are just starting to head up that steep curve.

Advanced smart cards containing a rather impressive 8 kilobytes of memory appeared in 1996, making them about as powerful as one of the old Apple II machines circa 1978. Then they jumped to 16K by the following year, then to 32K within just nine months after that and have more recently moved up to 64K, bringing them up to the level of the beloved Commodore64 computer, circa 1980. Meanwhile, the microprocessors embedded in the cards have been moving from 8-bit to 16-bit and, eventually, 32-bit.

Suddenly this tiny thing is becoming as powerful as a 386 PC, circa 1990.

"We've actually seen a quadrupling in memory within 18 months," says Tom Lebsack, director of multiple application services at Schlumberger (SHLUM-ber-jzay), the Montrouge, France-based corporation that has become the world's top maker of smart cards. "I think we're moving at twice the rate of Moore's Law, and I don't know what the limit is."

But the technology inside the card shouldn't matter—so long as they work, deliver tangible benefits to consumers, and provide a competitive advantage to the companies that issue them.

Among the first companies to do so have been resorts such as Club Med and cruise lines such as Holland America. In addition to doing away with the need to handle cash, which people on vacation do indeed crave, the card is also used to provide incentives to guests. The card, for instance, knows to charge you less for visiting a restaurant or a bar at off-peak hours. Or if you buy a certain amount of merchandise at the ship's store, it will provide free benefits, such as on-site film developing, right at the point of sale.

Other "closed communities," such as corporations, hospitals, colleges, and universities, have been issuing smart cards to their employees and customers. On campuses, the card is often the security device that students swipe through readers mounted at entrances, admitting them into only the buildings they are authorized to access and only at certain times—letting Joey Geekstein into the supercomputer lab at midnight and then onto the campus network itself, for instance, but preventing him from getting into a girl's dorm room. Plus, it manages information on a student's loan and course registration, and keeps track of how many dinners and lunches are left on the meal plan as well as loyalty points at the campus bookstore.

Since these cards are able to perform many tasks, marketing applications are joining the original security applications of smart cards. "The object is to change the behavior of the customer so that the relationship generates more revenue," says Jonathan Adams, Schlumberger's director of emerging markets. He calls this process "shift and lift" because it can transform the relationship companies have with their customers at the same time that it hoists sales.

Wacky Marketing Ideas

The number of ways that companies could use this technology to integrate the digital world and the real world are limited only by the imagination. A company that organizes trade shows, for instance, could not only promote its events at its website but pre-qualify potential attendees online, then upload a security code to attendees's smart cards that admits them into special sessions or the entire conference for free or at a discounted price. Such cards could hold any type of coupon or authentication—from concert tickets to sweepstakes certificates.

For all the billions of dollars of buying and selling already happening in the Web economy, far more business is lost when websites fail to convert browsers into paying customers. A recent survey by Jupiter Communications showed that while 35 percent of people who surf the Web did purchase something online within the past year, the remaining 65 percent didn't, even though the vast majority of those browsers said they did indeed use the Web to conduct research on products and services.

There is no doubt that vast business is transacted *offline* by people who may do online research. Companies usually can't determine how much business they could have captured but ended up losing to competitors. But smart cards enable companies for the first time to make a connection between the visit to a website and the consumer action or inaction that follows. By providing incentives and rewards online, then letting consumers download to their smart cards electronic certificates that represent those incentives, companies can now complete the loop—by getting more browsers to buy from the same company that offers free research tools.

Even as computers equipped with smart card readers make their way into the world, mainstream usage will surge only if marketing and customer service executives at thousands of companies create compelling applications. "The value of the smart card cannot even be discussed without evaluating the value of the marketing program behind it," says Schlumberger's Adams. "And the programs that work always begin with a wacky marketing idea."

Here's an early example: Customers of Edah, the largest grocery chain in the Netherlands, suddenly found themselves greeted one day by bright red computer kiosks inside the company's more than 300 stores. Called CardBoxes, the computers dispensed free smart cards and ran amusing interactive games and contests to encourage their use. The company's website did the same, offering free cards to be sent via mail.

For the Edah consumer, there are many benefits of having the card. First, it keeps track of loyalty points that can be redeemed for free food. Upon entering the store, cardholders insert their card into the terminal. Based on what that shopper has purchased in the past, specially tailored electronic coupons are downloaded onto the card and summarized on a printout that is instantly generated. After shopping, the shopper presents the card to the cashier, who swipes it through another card reader, which delivers the appropriate discounts and rewards.

For Edah, the benefits of smart cards revolve around target marketing. Every evening, special promotions are uploaded to the chain's network of kiosks, enticing different kinds of shoppers to buy different types of goods. Typically, Edah works with the packaged goods makers themselves to develop incentives to get customers to try new products. At the same time, Edah typically provides incentives for customers to buy the store's own brand of merchandise. These products are usually cheaper, but they also deliver higher profit margins to the store.

The experiment has been working. Within just a few months of offering the cards, more than 1.5 million Edah customers began using them. And Edah attributed an immediate 5 percent year-over-year boost in sales to its smart card program.

Hilton Hotels began using smart cards in a similar way, installing kiosks in the lobbies at many of its properties, and then began offering a special American Express smart card with 8 kilobytes of memory to some of its most frequent guests. The card keeps track of hotel, airline, and rental car loyalty points and enables travelers to bypass the check-in desk at Hilton hotels. Guests simply use their card to check in and out at the kiosk.

In the future, parts of these applications will happen at home or in cars, on computers that are equipped to read smart cards. Consumers will be able to download their customized grocery coupon list before they go to the store, or they'll be able to download certificates for free meals at the hotel before they go on their trip.

No one knows the magic formula for how much commerce customers will do online at home or at the office and how much will happen in person at thousands of locations. This strategy of integrating the two forms of commerce will likely yield all kinds of crazy new applications and an unpredictable range of responses on the part of consumers. But as we can see, companies of all types are starting to issue smart cards. Retailers, banks, airlines, hotels, computer makers, telephone companies, even popular Web traffic hubs such as Yahoo and Excite will all want to get in the game.

"The card is the key to all types of transaction services," says Philip Yen, senior vice president of chip cards at Visa International Inc. But executives at Visa, MasterCard, Schlumberger, and others also believe that consumers will want only one or two of these things, thus setting off a mad scramble among companies in many different industries as to whose card will integrate all different kinds of activities.

This fierce competition is happening at a time when the demand for such devices may explode. Dataquest Inc., a San Jose research firm, predicts the market worldwide for smart cards will jump from 941 million cards in 1997 to 4.7 billion cards in 2002. As usual, the first movers will have the upper hand in the race across the bridge between the cybersphere and the physical realm.

The World Is Your Network

Actually, smart cards are just one of many emerging technologies that integrate the physical and cyber worlds. New chips and software are now able to activate the senses of everyday objects and tie them together through the Web. "The world of the future is the world of personal networks," says Sun Microsystems technology chief Bill Joy.

He describes this network as one in which the vast majority of devices connected to it are non-computers, and one in which everything plugs in with utter ease. Computers, electronic devices, and smart objects should respond to human and business needs rather than sit there waiting for us to program them. "A community of devices will form and reform in a constant evolution," says Joy's colleague Mark Tolliver, president of Sun's embedded technology group.

For example, why aren't VCRs linked to the Web? If they were, they would know not to keep blinking 12:00 but to find out what time it is on their own—via an atomic clock on the Internet. By calling up the Web page of your VCR, you could program it to record a show from halfway around the world. Or why can't a book or a newspaper change into a *new* book or newspaper by receiving data via a wireless link to the Net? "Smart paper" technology now under development at the MIT Media Laboratory attempts to do just that. "The digital revolution so far has been for the computers, not the people," laments Neil Gershenfeld, a Media Lab professor.

Such technology adds a whole new dimension to consumer transactions. Say that you are faced with the choice of waiting in a line. Americans spend 101,369,863 hours per day doing so, according to Tom Heyman, author of *On an Average Day*. What if a consumer at an airport check-in line, at a crowded movie theater, or inside a retail store that is short on cashiers could simply pull out a palmtop gadget, call up a simple transaction page, and obtain their boarding pass, reserve their movie ticket, or purchase a tailored suit or piece of furniture on their own?

Actually, such technology now exists—using microwave radio. At the high end of the radio spectrum—at 2.4 gigahertz, to be precise—is a band of unregulated frequency specifically designated for personal networking services. Based on a three-chip radio transmitter and receiver, Motorola Corp.'s new Piano technology takes advantage of this frequency by transforming any gadget, from palm-size computers to cell phones to electronic wallets, into a two-way radio device.

As long as users stay within 10 feet of the designated Web server computer, they can perform specific tasks in this frequency band. "There is an enormous advantage to staying within short range," says Dave Leeper, Motorola's director of personal area networking. "We can move tens of megabytes to devices powered by penlight batteries." There's only one caveat: If you are standing next to a microwave oven that is cooking some soup, he says, your gadget may not work as advertised.

Such technology has the potential to disrupt entire industries. Retail chains that introduce this technology first can reassign their employees, reducing the number of cashiers and boosting the number of trained service people on the floor. The medical industry could also be transformed. Doctors and patients, for instance, could be given secure, password-protected access to medical records via the Web while in the hospital or their physicians' waiting room. In turn, hospitals and HMOs could reduce the cost of red tape and provide whole new levels of medical information services—a new market that Robertson, Stevens & Co. estimates will grow to $7 billion over the next five years.

The mainstream business applications of smart, connected objects are equally radical. Sun's connecting technology, called Jini, promises a world of devices that can detect one another and work together without specialized software. "We can enable your PalmPilot to print on a 10-year-old printer, with no operating systems, no drivers, no connectors, and no cables," says Sun chief operating officer Ed Zander. Jini is based on a simple 40-kilobyte communications program embedded on a tiny memory chip.

Eventually, he says, these chips will be built into any device, from camcorders to cars to shoes, at per-unit costs of about 10 cents. What this means is that people could be online while away from their desks or even their computers. Your own personal storehouse of files could be sitting on a server down the hall, and you could call it up in a conference room from a smart projection screen.

And so the possibilities for connecting all sorts of things to the Web are endless. For instance, since high-end cars already are equipped with built-in Global Positioning Satellite (GPS) receivers, car makers are now programming them to receive local weather and traffic data from the Web. A camcorder can be transformed into a Webcam. Link it to the Net, take it on vacation, and have your friends back home watch as you're having fun. "If there are a billion connected computers," says Ronald Whittier, a senior vice president of Intel, "there could be 10 billion connected peripheral devices."

Integrating the Enterprise

Perhaps the most dramatic yet overlooked capability of the Web is its potential to achieve total integration: the ability to blend what happens within an entire enterprise or to tie together the many actions occurring at a sprawling event.

Such possibilities are in the air on a breezy, Indian summer afternoon at the National Tennis Center in Flushing Meadows, New York, where ponytailed phenom Patrick Rafter is bouncing killer serves on the center court en route to his second straight U.S. Open singles title. But while the match is being played, there is just as much action going on underneath the pale-green surface, below the properly behaved, dressed-in-white crowd. Deep down in the basement level of the stadium, copper wires and strands of fiber optic cable course through the bowels of the arena, wind their way into the innards of the adjacent grandstand, and snake over to the 16 other courts scattered about the sprawling complex.

A tour of the facility reveals that there is far more computing and data communication going on here than tennis. Courtside photographers with digital cameras are feeding photo storage cards to Web designers who race back to banks of PCs and monitors. Webmasters are constantly uploading the photos, statistics, and match-by-match analysis to www.usopen.org. After every single point in every game, the new scores flow in real time to on-site Web servers that relay them to the online Java Scoreboard for the world to see. Robotically controlled courtside Webcams feed images to fans at home, where they can choose the camera angle. In another computer room inside the stadium, called the CyberCourt, the players themselves conduct live Web chats and check e-mail from far-flung family, friends, and fans. So far, Steffi Graf is the overwhelming leader, with more than 1,000 e-mailed good-luck tidings from around the world.

And, of course, there are plenty of IBM executives on hand to make sure that the whole world knows that they are running the show under an exclusive contract with the United States Tennis Association (USTA).

But why? "What's the business model here?" asks one reporter at a special all-day press tour of the facility. "Who pays who?" IBM executives make it clear that no cash changes hands between the USTA and IBM. The company gets no money from the USTA to install the on-site data network, develop the event's official website, and make sure that all the information systems associated with the U.S. Open are running smoothly. The effort requires a cast of hundreds of IBM employees and contractors over several months.

At first glance, it would seem that the USTA would be getting the better end of the bargain. Essentially, it is getting IBM to do all this work for it for free. But if you really dig deeper, IBM is making out like a bandit. "We provide valuable in-kind services for the visibility and the content," says Elizabeth (Eli) Primrose-Smith, a former swimming champ who is now IBM's vice president of worldwide Olympic and sports sponsorships. "We both contribute assets and share in the revenue." Still, Primrose-Smith is not even hinting at what the real benefits to IBM actually are.

To begin to see what's happening here, first realize that IBM has similar deals to integrate the information technology for the other three Grand Slam tennis events—Wimbledon and the French and Australian Open tournaments. It also runs the Olympics under a long-term contract, plus major golf events such as the PGA tour as well as pro basketball and hockey. And it does the information systems and website for a little thing called the Super Bowl, which drew a world record 3 million hits in just five hours in 1998.

IBM is almost always the highest-cost provider for these types of services—by a long shot—and it is remarkably willing to admit it. "We thought that [the Super Bowl site] would be a fairly minor undertaking, costing about $1 million," Primrose-Smith says with a shrug. "Boy, were we surprised." She says it cost way more than that.

For IBM, all this real-world integration of major sporting events works on two levels: First, IBM becomes the sole sponsor of the official event websites and experiences average click-through rates of 30 percent, which is more than ten times the average for a typical Web ad banner campaign. IBM couldn't possibly purchase the Web-using public's exclusive attention like that for any reasonable price.

To boot, these sites have incredible global research. For the U.S. Open site, IBM received visitors from every country on Earth that has a domain name suffix, more than 100 nations in total. With vast time-zone differences, live television cannot cover all events in their entirety, especially for sprawling mega-events such as the Olympics. But the Web can. It can cover them in depth, with unique features and statistics that people cannot get on television. The Web can serve up stats on the "impact force" of a football player, or the "game-flow diagram" of a basketball matchup, or a baseball batter's "hot zone." "The idea is to deliver an experience that complements TV," says Jeff Ramminger, an IBM interactive media executive.

Typically, IBM shares in the ticket and merchandise revenue sold online. But the intangible factor leads to far greater rewards. IBM, in effect, owns these events and is able to use technology to direct attention to itself. Given the demographics of some of these sports, especially golf and tennis, this is a potential gold mine. And, as IBM can attest, all this effort pays for itself many times over in the new business it attracts.

This is where classic, old-fashioned business comes into play. When IBM invites a CEO from a potential client to one of these events and shows him or her how real-world integration can be accomplished, the real benefits begin to flow. That is modern business practiced at its highest level. In catered luxury boxes. On golf courses. In exclusive clubs. On sports junkets. This is real bonding in real time. This is leveraging a unique experience to win the favor of real people. Yes, there's the Internet. But the old-boy net is still just as powerful, if not more so. "Sports are not a hard thing to talk about with senior executives," Ramminger says with a wink. "It works to draw analogies to their business."

The not-so-hidden secret about IBM is that it hardly even does any of this work itself. It subcontracts major parts of most jobs. These subcontractors get paid well and on time, but they have to, in effect, make believe they are with IBM and sign contracts that keep their name in the background. IBM takes all the credit. "We hire the right people and integrate them," says Ramminger.

As time goes by, IBM is collecting critical know-how. It has learned, for instance, that security takes on heightened importance at such events—witness the stabbing of Monica Seles in 1993, the walloping of Nancy Kerrigan's kneecap in 1994, and the bombing during the 1996 Olympic Games in Atlanta. That's why IBM filters incoming e-mail for potential loonies. It has also learned from embarrassing mistakes. During the Atlanta games, for instance, it was running TV ads touting how reliable its systems were at the same time glitches were preventing it from relaying key scores to the media. IBM executives will also admit that they have underestimated the cost, time, and manpower needed to ace these big sports ventures.

Yet many of these mistakes are easily forgotten. Pretty soon others will have a hard time matching IBM's integration skills. But competitors would be foolish to cede this strategy to IBM. Instead of just running banner ads on a general-purpose website, integrating high-profile events can become a powerful sales and marketing tool for any technology-oriented company.

"The sports calendar is getting divvied up into unique events," says Mark Hardie, an entertainment industry analyst with Forrester Research. "And more sports are coming to the Web to take advantage of this." There's the Super Bowl in January. College Basketball's "March Madness." World Cup Soccer in June. The Summer Olympics every fourth year. Wimbledon in August. Ryder Cup golf every other September. The baseball playoffs and World Series in October. Scattered about the year are world-class events that have loyal but highly segmented followers all over the world, in competition such as sailing, bicycle racing, auto racing, and chess.

Corporations need to draw lessons from these live events. Like the world of sports, the world of business has online and offline components that must be integrated in real time. All your events, all your employees, all your sales channels have a component that ties in with Web commerce.

That's why when you now ask IBM executives what portion of the company's total revenue (which now tops $80 billion annually) comes from e-business initiatives, they will reply: "All of it." In a very short time, e-business has become the number-one opportunity in the information technology industry. But despite the central message of IBM's e-business marketing blitz—that any business can be turned into an e-business—most companies don't exactly get the point. Their Web operations don't tie in well with what is happening in the real world or with their other sales, marketing, and service channels. They're not using computers to support people and using people to support computers. Instead, most companies still treat the Web as a stand-alone function, detached from everything else.

Everyone from the CEO on down needs to take a higher-level view of the digital enterprise and become an integral player in it. They need to integrate their personal computers, smart cards, digital telephones, palmtop computing devices, and real-world stores, business units, subsidiaries, campuses, and special events into a cohesive whole. In the end, the most important part of Web commerce isn't the technology; it's the people. The enterprises that fail to cross-pollinate their Web ventures with what the rest of the company does on a daily basis may find themselves among their industry's most endangered species.

EXECUTIVE SURVIVAL GUIDE:
REAL-WORLD INTEGRATION

▶ Tie together all forms of distribution with the Web. Make sure your Web venture doesn't exist in a parallel universe, run by people who have nothing to do with the rest of your company.

▶ Set up effective "feedback loops" between your different business channels. For retailers, that means using your brick-and-mortar stores to encourage use of the unique features of your website, using your website to promote traffic to in-store events, and using your catalogs to promote both.

▶ Issue smart cards as the missing link between Web commerce and traditional commerce. Smart cards can store special coupons, tickets, or frequent-buyer points downloaded from the Web, redeemable in person.

▶ Encourage the portability of Web commerce by making sure that your website supports access not just from personal computers but also from palm-size devices, digital telephones, car computers, and kiosks located in stores, airports, libraries, and other public spaces.

▶ In the end, you must evolve into the ultimate hybrid enterprise—finding new ways to integrate everything that your company does online with everything that it does offline.

EPILOGUE

THE GREAT SORTING

Evolution has produced an animal with a neck so long that it can dine from the treetops. The same process has also yielded a frail, vulnerable creature that can outrun just about anything. The giraffe is strange, while the gazelle is graceful. But both are incredibly successful—among the tiny percentage of all species that have survived millennia after millennia by evolving traits that give them an edge. Likewise, the mutating digital business environment will most assuredly produce enterprises that will seem quite exceptional or rather bizarre by today's standards. "In the future, there will be even weirder business models," says Tim Berners-Lee, the physicist who conceived the World Wide Web in 1989 and gave it its name. "We won't just be doing obvious things like taking mail order and putting it on the Net."

Even if we can't foresee future variations among corporate species, we can get a glimpse of where we are going by returning to the original visionaries who drove the Web's early acceptance. Shortly after placing his "global hypertext system" on the Internet, Berners-Lee witnessed an explosion that can only be compared to the replication bomb of life. Eventually, usage of the Web will "saturate the developed world," he says, "to the point where it can be compared to television."

His comparison is to the pervasiveness of the television, not to the way the technology is used. The Web is most powerful not as a mass medium, he suggests, but rather a means for organizing communities, niche markets, and teams within companies. "I'm less happy with the incentive for reaching a global audience," adds Berners-Lee. "The good news is that intranets are bringing the technology back into corporations to be used as a group tool."

In the future, he says, the Web will be more fun, will blend better into everyday life, and will be something that doesn't even require computers as we've come to know them. "Your kids will be rummaging through boxes of breakfast cereal," he muses, "and they'll say: 'What is this?' And they'll pull it out and unroll it, and it will be magnetic, and they'll put it on the refrigerator, and start browsing the Web with it."

Agreeing with this vision is Marc Andreessen, the Netscape cofounder who developed the first commercial Web browser software. "Every device that has a sliver of silicon in it will end up connected to the Net," he says. Cars, clothing, kitchen appliances, and camcorders will have their own Web addresses.

The costs of computing and communications will continue to decline. "PC prices will go to zero and even below zero," Andreessen predicts. "What if telecom companies start handing out PCs for free to sign you up for Internet service and show you ads?" Actually, this is something that has already happened and it greatly disturbs Berners-Lee. He sees a danger in bundling everything together this way. "I was brought up on the *Times* [of London]," he says, "which people buy for its editorial independence." But nowadays, "the search button on the browser no longer provides an objective search but a commercial one. Hardware comes with software that sells rather than informs."

Andreessen, meanwhile, foresees a convergence—but not so much in the technological sense, as in the PC, TV, and phone consolidating into one Swiss Army knife design. The greater convergence will occur in a business context. "It's becoming brutal," he says. "In financial services, we'll have banks, brokerages, mutual fund companies, insurance companies, financial newspapers, even software developers all competing with one another." Industries will become integrated and cross-bred to the point that "you'll click on your browser and get offered a lowfat latté with a mutual fund."

As markets evolve, Andreessen expects a further spread of the entrepreneurial fever that he and legions of others caught in the Web's early days. "A new company springs up out of nowhere and gets 1 percent of a very large industry, and the stock market rewards that with a giant valuation," he observes. As a result, two primal emotions will continue to govern behavior: Greed will motivate companies to reap the rewards of changing an entire industry. And fear will motivate those enterprises that wish to avoid getting trampled.

Berners-Lee is likewise in awe of the financial ramifications of the technology he unleashed. "There is a fascinating relationship between links and money," he notes. "Everyone is so excited at the moment that they are thinking of new businesses to start five times a day."

"I'm very excited too," he adds. Like many others, he's been surprised by the financial markets' response to the Web. Yet he maintains that he's "not going to predict gloom," even though others claim that the Web economy is nothing more than a speculative bubble. The Web itself, he says, is an "equilibrium" that will tend to balance itself out. And evolution only moves forward. "We're not going to do a U-turn and go back to where we were in 1991."

Shaping Your Organizational DNA

In the early part of the twentieth century, capitalist Alfred Sloan ran General Motors like a colossal machine comprising distinct parts, each serving a different function. Based on Newton's concept of a clockwork universe and Adam Smith's notion of division of labor, that type of command-and-control hierarchy served as the model for running all large enterprises, from the army to old IBM. But the aging industrial model of management is dysfunctional in the Web economy and in the new world of work at large. At the cusp of the new millennium, the mechanical mold is on the rust heap of history.

Sprouting in its place is a more fit metaphor based on Darwinian evolution. "We need to create biological organizations," the computer interface pioneer Alan Kay told me a few years back. A former Apple Computer research fellow, Kay has more recently been helping to shape the Walt Disney Corporation's new biology, as one of its "imagineers." If you think of every company as an evolving economic organism, he says, then each must possess "organizational DNA." This radical notion, already referred to a few times throughout this book, is no longer especially new or original. But the exciting development is that it is finally being put into action across many different species of enterprises.

Under this biological model, an organization is shaped by coded instructions that determine what it is—and those instructions are often embedded most simply in the company's mission statement. Each employee must be a smart cell with a full set of knowledge, talents, and skills necessary for executing the mission. All these cells are joined by a communications network, not unlike a central nervous system, that is too complex to be controlled centrally. New cells must be trained quickly to replace the ones that leave. In this sense, the organism moves through time, all the while learning, adapting, and rejuvenating itself. And if you change the organizational DNA, it will yield an entirely new organism.

Organizational DNA, therefore, is a blueprint based on the goals and values of the company—its purpose in life beyond that of mere survival. With this blueprint, employees can create the processes needed to achieve those goals—business models, management structures, and strategic relationships.

As noted at the book's beginning, evolution among these biological enterprises takes time to produce lessons, results, and outcomes. We can already look around and learn from the major conflicts, the successes, the failures, the turning points in the Web's early, chaotic years. Of course, we cannot claim to know with any degree of certainty where we're headed. But as we pass through new generations of business models and management tactics, the enterprises with the fittest organizational DNA will tend to grow stronger, while the weaker ones will tend to die out.

Time itself, therefore, produces a great sorting. With each generation, time acts as a sieve that filters out bad genes and passes on the good ones. Think back to the primitive Web of 1995 or so, for instance, and try to remember what it looked like and which companies seemed destined for success back then. Many organisms with strong organizational DNA have indeed gone on to dominate their markets. Other promising ones turned out to have bad genes, faulty organizational DNA, unfit business models. Thus, they died young or were swallowed up by a rival. Still others survived out of sheer randomness, fluke fortune, and ample assistance from venture capitalists, benefactors, and part-ners. "Genes can buy their way through the sieve," writes Richard Dawkins, Oxford University's esteemed Darwinian zoologist. But not for very long.

So how do we determine which companies have the best chance at prosperity and longevity? Can we judge by their stock prices or other outward signs? Evolutionists would caution strongly against doing so. The principle of survival of the fittest doesn't mean that anything that survives is necessarily fit. One can prosper for a time even as extinction lies just ahead. Darwin just meant that certain variations confer a natural advantage. "It's not success that makes good genes," notes Dawkins. "It's good genes that make success." Good genes are simply more likely than bad ones to be replicated, to be passed on, to survive.

The great sorting isn't just happening among Internet start-ups but among those in the larger corporate world. And the un-precedented merger frenzy—in industries ranging from comput-ing and telecommunications to insurance and banking to autos and oil—is both a symptom and a cause of the shakeout. CEOs often refer to mergers as "marriages," thus extending the metaphor of sexual combination. After such marriages are consummated, divi-sions are folded into one another, just as genes combine, and cer-tain traits and activities are abandoned. The individual parents fade away and give way to the new offspring. Hopefully, the combined enterprise is stronger than its ancestors.

Usually, it makes for a new organizational DNA. In this sense, combined entities such as DaimlerChrysler, Citigroup, and AT&T (after merging with cable giant TCI) suddenly need to have as much in common with Dell Computer, E*Trade, and America Online as they do with their own parents. The big seem to be get-ting bigger. But the Web, in part, is causing old machinelike structures among the giants to be broken down. "If you don't break it, someone else will" and "creative destruction" have become the new corporate mantras.

Large enterprises have learned that they don't have to control their entire food chains. As detailed earlier, the new world of network production has enabled them to farm work out over the Net to symbiotic species. Partnerships and equity investments have replaced the old idea of developing dedicated divisions to do everything inside the firm. As a result, corporations now have far fewer employees but far more people working for them. Such enterprises are indeed becoming more responsive, more innovative, more adaptable.

Darwin's Remarkable Theory

In the early years of the Web economy, the prevailing view among those of us caught up in the day-to-day doings of the digital revolution has been this: Web start-ups confer enormous advantages over their land-based brethren. The growth potential on this new, empty terrain was unlimited. The cost of doing business on the Web was enormously lower than that of land-bound enterprises that had to maintain bricks, mortar, and other tangible assets. The global reach of the Web enabled the smallest start-ups to sell into hundreds of countries without actually being there. And such start-ups were without the baggage of outmoded business models and cumbersome, slow-footed organizations.

All of this has largely been true. Yet it is becoming less and less so. The relentless battle for attention among rival Web start-ups has produced a situation in which a stand-alone website is at a distinct and growing *disadvantage.* We are now coming to realize that a retailer on the Web benefits greatly from being integrated with actual stores. Web enterprises that sell expensive and complex products and services can use the help of expert human salespeople. As this kind of real-world integration becomes a fact of business life, it will continue to set off a mad game of musical chairs, a scramble among the species for partners, leading to more and more hybrid enterprises.

The early excitement of Web commerce has also thrown many of us for a loop. Chalk it up to the pre-millennial madness of the crowd. But the constant bombardment of change has led to a predicament in which rational thinking has become intertwined with the irrational. Rational businesses are the ones that are valued based on their earnings and the growth of their earnings. Irrational businesses are the ones valued, or vastly overvalued, based on nothing so tangible as revenue or profits but rather on their sheer potential, the story that they tell. Often, this potential is greatly misunderstood, exaggerated, or subject to extreme wishful thinking.

Digital Darwinism involves the process of distinguishing between the two, sorting out the rational from the irrational. As each successive generation of Web commerce passes, there will be more rational companies and fewer irrational ones, more fit business models and fewer unfit ones. In the future, there may be no such thing as an Internet company. The Internet is becoming so important that all companies will eventually become Internet companies. And Internet start-ups will have less and less of an initial advantage. But that doesn't mean that today's Internet start-ups are all operating within a bubble that will pop. It may just mean that many of the more traditional species are vastly *undervalued*.

Which brings us back to Charles Darwin himself. Darwin's idea of evolution by natural selection was indeed only just a theory—he was unable to prove his theory outright, even though he had spent years gathering circumstantial evidence through observation. It struck him that all species must have come from a common ancestor and evolved, adapted, and varied over time in different directions due to many different environmental factors. But he didn't know precisely how organisms passed on traits to new generations. Mendel's discovery of the basic laws of heredity weren't publicized until well after Darwin published *The Origin of Species*. And Watson and Crick didn't discover the double helix of DNA until 1953. These developments have confirmed Darwin's basic theory as scientific fact, even though it is still not universally taken as gospel.

We now know that genes are passed along via precise, embedded numerical codes. Just as computers operate on *binary* codes, usually represented by 1s and 0s, biological beings operate on *quadrary* codes, usually represented by As, Gs, Cs, and Ts. In both cases, long strings of digits can convey any type of information in infinite complexity. Computers execute software programs of mind-boggling complexity, while cells execute genetic programs that are even more elaborate. In this sense, Darwinism has always been digital. Yet Darwin himself could not have known that.

Theories of evolution in the Web economy are likewise difficult to prove. We may not know what the future holds. Only by observing, like Darwin, how economic species have evolved and where we are now, can we recognize the patterns of what works, what doesn't, and why. For now, all we know is that market forces are ensuring that life in the Web economy is evolving in a self-organizing but unplanned manner, with no one company in control, and no one system of beliefs in a dominant position.

It's quite likely that the number of people online will surpass 1 billion in just a few short years. All these individuals will control not only what they see and do but what they create. The Web is a subjective universe of information, ideas, and commerce. As more and more people log on, "the complex web of relations" that Darwin referred to takes on a whole new meaning. Our creations and our work will perhaps become more interesting, more challenging, and less repetitive than ever imagined. Individually, each of our successes will be based on constant innovation. Collectively, we'll be creating entirely new forms of enterprises with surprising new traits and characteristics. "From so simple a beginning," Darwin concluded, "endless forms, most beautiful and most wonderful have been and are being evolved." In other words, one thing is certain: We will continue to amaze ourselves.

ACKNOWLEDGMENTS

In the spring of 1997, soon after *Webonomics* was published, I began gathering string to write about the next phase of Web commerce. But what could possibly happen next? Everyone was rushing on-line. Everyone seemed to agree that the Internet was somehow revolutionizing business. Everyone seemed to know about the hype and the chaos and "the bubble." Everyone knew that everyone couldn't succeed—that there would be winners and losers. But what determines success? What were the most powerful business models? Who was best adapting to the new environment? And who was totally oblivious to the fact that things worked differently in a world in which everyone had instant access to information and in which no one could control behavior? All signs pointed one way: that the Web economy had to be Darwinian.

Thanks to the nice ladies at the Brookline Public Library who pointed me toward the books on the subject. As I opened these old volumes, I found some so dusty that they induced fits of sneezing. After reading some of Darwin's own works, as well as those from neo-Darwinists with names such as Dawkins and Dennett, I was convinced that Darwinism was indeed an appropriate metaphor for understanding evolution in the Web economy. Darwin himself acknowledged that natural selection was merely a "metaphorical expression," a phrase that shouldn't be taken too literally. The same is true with digital Darwinism. In addition, Darwinism shouldn't be confused with social Darwinism, a set of misapplied theories and idiocies that Darwin himself never espoused.

Around the time that the new title was affirmed by my editor, I moved into an office and started writing and interviewing and surfing. Thanks to the guys at the Metropolitan Collection Bureau, who subleased me the office space—provided that I paid the rent on time. Thanks to John the postman, who doubles as a daytrader. At about 2:45 P.M. each day, he brings catalogs, bills, credit card pitches, and fantastic tips on tech stocks about which he admittedly knows just enough to be really, really dangerous to his family's finances. "Seven-dollar commissions," he kept telling me. "Can't beat it."

Thanks to Jonathan Alsop, Mary Riendeau, and everyone at The World, my trusty Internet service provider and gracious website host, which just happens to be headquartered down the hall from my aforementioned office. Very little thanks to Bell Atlantic, which has been charging me a 1.6 cent per minute "business rate" to dial down that very same hall.

In this age of e-commerce, we sometimes lose perspective and fail to recognize the indispensability of face-to-face contact, especially when it involves good food and drink. Yet we all know this: Ya gotta eat! In recognition of this most underappreciated force in the business world, I want to thank everyone who shared meals with me and sparked ideas over the past two years:

James Roach of Fort Point Partners at the now defunct Blue Wave; Bob Buday of the Bloom Group at Sonsie; Robert Olson of

Virtual Vineyards at Cybersmith; Ryan Mathews, then of the Progressive Grocer, at the Park Plaza; Philip Yen, Janet Pruitt, and Ryan Mikolasik from Visa International at Giannino's in Charles Square; Larry Downes of Diamond Technology Partners at Grappa in Chicago; Alastair Rolfe of Penguin UK and Mark Ellingham of Rough Guides at Pegs in Covent Garden; George Zinkhan and Srini Reddy of the University of Georgia at that funky little shack in Athens; Amy Bruckman of Georgia Tech at Mambo; Sunil Gupta of the University of Michigan of Ann Arbor's Charley's; Dana Blankenhorn at Atlanta's Max Lager's; Russ Neuman of Penn's Annenberg School at Sitar India; Morgan Jones of UNC-Chapel Hill and John McCann of Duke at the Governor's Inn in Research Triangle Park; David Morrison of the World Economic Forum at Henrietta's Table; Michael Wolff at Virgil's; Bill Morris of Dell Computer at Gilligan's in downtown Austin; Chas Humphreyson, Loreen Costello, Bob Wieneke, and Jordan Olshansky at that BBQ joint in Dallas; Michael Davis of MicroAge at Al Forno in Providence; Alan Alper of Gomez Advisors at the Coolidge Corner Clubhouse; Jeffrey Leopold of Sapient and Jeffrey Rayport of Harvard Business School, each at Zaftig's; John Bennett of PictureTalk at Spettro in Oakland; Melody Kean Haller of the Antenna Group, Brewster Kahle of Alexa, and John Helm of AllApartments.com at LuLu's in SoMa; Andrew Collins and Aldo Castaneda of Thingworld.com at Seattle's Best Coffee; Robert Jennings of Mediconsult at Starbucks; Jarvis Coffin and everyone at Burst Media at the Burlington Marriot; Erik Brynjolfsson of MIT, Neil Budde of The Wall Street Journal Interactive, Annette Tonti of BlueStreak.com, and Margaret Heffernan of ZineZone, each at the Sail Loft in Cambridge; Ed Mullen of CMG at Johnny's Luncheonette; Dan Kamas, Chad Roffers, Lisa Walker, and the US West Dex team for having the guts to take a Bostonian out for seafood in Minneapolis (at the Blue Point Oyster Bar), as well as

ACKNOWLEDGMENTS

Jim Smith, Robin Baca, and Jeffrey Tarr at the Macaroni Grill in Denver; Theo Snijders, Ernst Fuld, and Forrester's Emily Green at the Hilton Amsterdam, as well as the entire gang at the Leidseplein's Grande Café (don't miss the pasta bolognese); Hans-Jürgen Croissant and company with Burda Media at Munich's Seehaus in the Englischen Garten; Ralph DiMuccio, Greg Memo, and Scott Holder of Compaq Computer at The County Line in Houston, as well as Kjell Hegstad, Gerry Campbell, and the group at the Compaq campus cafeteria, where you can get custom meals made to order—the ultimate in personalization! Plus, constant thanks to everyone at the Bottega Fiorentina and Anna's Taqueria for my daily sustenance.

Thanks to the editors who have worked with me on stories and helped hone ideas for this book: Brad Wieners at *Wired,* Tim Race at the *New York Times,* Pegeen Hopkins and Paul Carroll at *Context,* and Jonathan Weber and John Battelle at the *Industry Standard.*

Special thanks to the dozens of people who agreed to be interviewed. Too numerous to be mentioned here, they are acknowledged in the Notes section.

Undying thanks to Elyse Cheney at SJG, and to Lauren Marino, Ann Campbell, and the rest of the team at Broadway Books, who came through once again in short time.

Finally, mucho gratitude to my friends and family for their love and support, especially to Michaela and Lily, and to Amy, who is always there for me.

APPENDIX

A DIRECTORY OF

BUSINESS MODELS

The following is a selection of Web enterprises that practice at least one of the seven survival strategies detailed in this book. It's not meant as a complete listing, but rather a sample of the range of companies that are putting these business models into action.

Solution Branding

Ask Jeeves—type any question,
  click "ask." .... askjeeves.com
Autobytel.com—car buying
  service .... autobytel.com
Amazon.com—book, CD, gift
  recommendations.......................... amazon.com
Bike Finder—*Bicycling* mag's
  search service .... bike-finder.com
ComputerShopper—ZDNet's
  PC recommendations .... computershopper.com
CruiseAssist—which boat to take .... cruiseassist.com

Egift—personal gift finder .... egift.com

Etoys—toy finder .... etoys.com

FundFilter—E*Trade's mutual
fund selection guide .... fundfilter.etrade.com

HomeAdvisor—home buying,
financing .... homeadvisor.msn.com

The Knot—wedding guide.............. theknot.com

LifeServe—life event planning
software .... lifeserve.com

Quicken—financial advice and
tools .... quicken.com

ShopLink—groceries and chores ...... shoplink.com

Streamline—groceries and chores .... streamline.com

Virtual Vinyards—expert wine
advice .... virtualvin.com

Wedding Channel—big day
planning .... weddingchannel.com

Yahoo! .... yahoo.com

Dynamic Pricing

ArbiNet—long-distance phone
minutes exchange .... arbinet.com

Auction Network—used cars........... aucnet.com

Band-X—trading telecom
capacity .... bandx.com

Capesaffron—phone minutes .... capesaffron.com

Ebay—person-to-person auctions..... ebay.com

Energymarket—Southern
California Gas.............................. energymarket.com

E-World Auction—old books
maps, manuscripts....................... eworldauction.com

Fairmarket—excess electronics .... fairmarket.com

Fastparts—electronic parts .... fastparts.com

FirstAuction—jewelry, household
   items, electronics......................... firstauction.com

iEscrow—secure money holder
   for auctions.................................. iescrow.com

Interxion—long-distance
   exchange..................................... interxion.com

Internet Auction List—guide to
   thousands of auctions................... internetauctionlist.com

Live Bid—vintage car auction .... livebid.com

National Transportation
   Exchange—buy and sell
   truck space .... nte.net

Narrowline—Web ad space
   auction .... narrowline.com

Onsale—excess PC, travel
   inventor...................................... onsale.com

Priceline—name your airfare .... priceline.com

Rate Exchange—telephone
   minutes .... ratexchange.com

Sotheby's—upscale auctions............. sothebys.com

Affiliate Networking

Amazon.com Associates Program..... amazon.com/associates

Artuframe—artworks and custom
   framing .... artuframe.com

Be Free—affiliate net software......... befree.com

CDnow Cosmic Credit..................... cdnow.com

Digital River—software shop .... digitalriver.com

The Lobster Net .... thelobsternet.com

LinkShare—affiliate program
   management................................. linkshare.com

Omaha Steaks—meat by mail.......... omahasteak.com

The One-And-Only Network—
dating service .... oneandonly.com

Refer-It—guide to affiliate
programs .... refer-it.com

Shades.com—sunglasses................... shades.com

Swiss Army Depot—pocket
knives... swissarmydepot.com

Thingworld.com—cool animated
icons... thingworld.com

Value Bundling

@Home—high speed net access
bundled with search and
content .... home.com

America Online .... aol.com

AppNet—bundle of e-business
services .... appnet.com

CBS Sportsline.............................. sportsline.com

Consumer Reports .... consumerreports.org

Disney's Daily Blast—kid stuff........ dailyblast.com

ESPN SportsZone .... espn.com

Every CD—record club .... everycd.com

The Microsoft Network .... home.microsoft.com

NetMarket—subscription-based
wholesale shopping site .... netmarket.com

New York Today—arts and
entertainment guide from the
New York Times .... nytoday.com

The Street—investment
analysis.. thestreet.com

The Wall Street Journal
   Interactive Edition........................wsj.com

Network Production

Apple Computer............................. apple.com
CDnow—you select the songs .... cdnow.com
Chip Shot Golf—
   custom-made clubs .... chipshotgolf.com
Cisco Corp..................................... cisco.com
Compaq Computer .... compaq.com
Creative Parties Online—
   made-to-order decorations
   and party gear............................. party-creations.com
Dell Computer .... dell.com
Greentree—personal vitamin
   tablets .... greentree.com
Intel Corp...................................... intel.com
iPrint—make your own
   stationary.................................... iprint.com
Manhattan Custom Tackle—
   fishing kits .... fishdoc.com
MotherNature.com—custom
   vitamins .... mothernature.com
Seven Cycles—custom-built bikes ... sevencycles.com
Swatch... swatch.com

Cybermediation

All Apartments—rental listings ...... allapartments.com
Aviation Week marketplace............. aircraftbuyer.com
BizTravel.com—business travel
   services .... biztravel.com

Classmates—high-school chum
    locator .... classmates.com

CyberHomes—home listings .... cyberhomes.com

Discover Brokerage Direct .... discoverbrokerage.com

DLJ Direct—brokerage services .... dljdirect.com

E*trade .... etrade.com

Expedia—travel services .... expedia.com

Home Portfolio—home
    improvement .... homeportfolio.com

ImproveNet—contractor finder .... improvenet.com

Instill's e•store—restaurant food
    purchasing .... instill.com

Mediconsult—health and
    pharmaceutical services .... mediconsult.com

Metalsite.com—trade exchange
    for Wierton steel .... metalsite.com

Merrill Lynch .... ml.com

Monster Board—job listings and
    employment services .... monsterboard.com

NECX—corporate purchasing
    network for electronics and
    computers .... necx.com

NextCard—online credit card
    approval and balance transfers .... nextcard.com

Owners Network—for-sale by
    owner homes .... owners.com

PlanetAll—contact management ..... planetall.com

Realtor.com—home sales .... realtor.com

Internet Truckstop—freight
    matching service .... truckstop.com

Charles Schwab .... eschwab.com

Travelocity .... travelocity.com

Real-World Integration

Agranat Systems—embedded
  Web connection circuitry for
  appliances .... agranat.com
Brookline Booksmith .... brooklinebooksmith.com
CMG Direct—integration of
  Web and direct marketing .... cmgdirect.com
Edah—Dutch grocery stores .... edah.nl
The Gap .... gap.com
IBM—integration solutions .... ibm.com
Kinkos—document services .... kinkos.com
Motorola—smart devices .... mot.com
Netpulse—Web browsing
  while you work out .... netpulse.com
OnStar—car location technology ..... onstar.com
PalmPilot—3Com's info
  appliances .... palmpilot.com
Peeping Moe—webcam guide .... peepingmoe.com
Proton World—smart cards from
  Visa and AmEx .... protonworld.com
REI—outdoor clothing and gear ..... rei.com
Schlumberger—maker of smart
  cards .... schlumberger.com/smartcards
Smart Routes—traffic cams .... smartroutes.com
Sun Microsystems—Jini
  connection technology .... sun.com/jini
US West Dex—Internet
  yellow pages .... uswestdex.com
Victoria's Secret .... victoriassecret.com
Webcam Central .... webcamcentral.com

NOTES

INTRODUCTION

Pages 3–20: Charles Darwin quotes are from *The Origin of Species—By Means of Natural Selection or the Preservation of Favoured Races in the Struggle for Life,* 6th ed., from Oxford University Press. (The first edition was published in 1859 and the sixth, the final one to appear during in Darwin's life, was published in 1872.)

Pages 6–7: Revenue figures for the travel industry from the American Society of Travel Agents.

Pages 6–12: Electronic commerce projections are general consensus forecasts from Jupiter Communications, International Data Corp., Forrester Research, and ActivMedia Inc.

Page 9: Venture capital figures from Morgan Stanley Dean Witter Discover Inc.

Quote from Vinod Khosla, a partner with Kleiner Perkins, from the *New York Times,* October 27, 1998, p. C6.

Pages 9, 14: Interview with Chas B. Humphreyson of HO2

Partners, a Dallas-based Internet venture capital firm, September 1998.

Page 9: Interview with Stephen G. Hall of Prospect Street Ventures, a New York venture firm, October 1998, at the Venture Market East conference, Cambridge, Massachussetts.

Page 10: Interview with Michael Barach, a former partner with Bessemer Ventures, September 1998. (Barach has since become chief executive officer of MotherNature.com, an online retailer of vitamins and supplements.)

Page 12: "Tulipmania.com," by James J. Cramer, *Time,* August 3, 1998, p. 77.

Pages 14–15: Kinetic Strategies Inc. estimated that cable modem service was commercially available to more than 11 million homes in North America on May 1, 1998, and that cable operators had landed more than 200,000 Internet subscribers.

Figures correlating online shopping with years online are from the Georgia Tech Internet user survey, April 1998, available at www.gvu.gatech.edu/user-surveys/

Page 15: Advertising share figures from "The Great Portal Shakeout," a 1998 report by Forrester Research.

Page 16: Quote by Yahoo's Tim Koogle from the *Boston Globe,* November 25, 1998, p. D1.

Pages 16–17: Morgan Stanley's Internet Retail Report, by Mary Meeker et al., May 28, 1997.

CHAPTER ONE

Pages 22–23: Interviews with Andrew Parkinson, CEO of Peapod, October 1997 and April 1998.

Pages 23, 25, 30–31: Interviews with Ryan Mathews, former editor of *Progressive Grocer,* June 1997 and April 1998.

Pages 21–22: "Best and Worst: Wall Street has floated 590

new stock issues in '97, raising $38 billion from U.S. investors; A pretty healthy year," by Scott Reeves, *Barron's,* December 15, 1997, p. 39. The story says that Peapod's stock had lost 69 percent of its value to date since going public at $16 in June 1997.

Pages 24–26: Interview with Daniel Nissan, founder of NetGrocer, April 1998. Financial data from NetGrocer prospectus. Also see: "Cybertales of woe: A look at two online ventures that didn't make it," by Andrea Petersen, the *Wall Street Journal,* December 7, 1998, p. R18. The story says that "NetGrocer Inc. recently put its IPO on hold, fired its chief executive and laid off a bunch of employees."

Page 26: Cendant was in the news constantly from April through October 1998 for its accounting scandal. "Investors Seek to Oust Chairman of Cendant on Fraud Disclosure," the *Wall Street Journal,* July 16, 1998, was typical of the headlines.

Pages 26–31: Interview with Timothy DeMello, CEO of Streamline, October 1998.

Pages 32–38: Interview with Stuart Agres, vice president of Young & Rubicam, September 1998. "Changing Need for Brands," by Stuart Agres and Tony Dubitsky, *Journal of Advertising Research* (January/February 1996.)

Pages 32–34, 41: Interview with David Aaker, of University of California, Berkeley, April 1998. Some brand history references are from his books, *Managing Brand Equity* (Free Press, 1991) and *Building Strong Brands* (Free Press, 1996).

Page 32: *Webonomics* (Broadway Books, 1997), by Evan I. Schwartz, p. 56.

"Branding on the Net," by Ellen Neuborne et al., *BusinessWeek,* November 9, 1998.

Pages 34, 38: Interview with Mark Dempster, of USWeb/CKS, February 1998.

Page 39: Mark Andreessen, keynote speech at the annual meeting of the Massachusetts Software Council, April 1998.

Page 40: Andreessen's e-mail message to Steve Case quoted in the *Boston Globe,* November 23, 1998, p. C6.

Pages 41–42: Jerry Yang, Yahoo cofounder, quote from keynote at Harvard University's Cyberposium, February 1998. Yahoo CEO Timothy Koogle's quote from talk at the *Wall Street Journal*'s Technology Summit, October 1998.

CHAPTER TWO

Pages 44–50, 63: Interview with Marcus de Ferranti, cofounder of Band-X, October 1998.

Pages 48–49: "The One to Watch: Band-X's bandwidth brokerage threatens the major telcos," by Christina Stubbs, *The Red Herring* magazine (October 1998).

Pages 50–54: Interview with Jay S. Walker, founder of Walker Digital and Priceline.com, August, 1998.

Pages 55–56: Final quotes from Jay Walker are from "The Priceline.com is Right," by David Noonan, *The Industry Standard,* January 4, 1999, p. 61.

Pages 60–62: Interview with Jerry Kaplan, CEO of Onsale Inc., February 1998.

Pages 63–65: Interview with Pierre Omidyar, founder of eBay, February 1998.

Pages 63–65: Interview with Susan Grant, vice president of the National Consumers League, February 1998.

Pages 66–67: Interview with Oliver Selfridge, formerly with MIT Lincoln Labs, January 1994.

Pages 67–69: Interview with Jeffrey Kephart, IBM research scientist, September 1998. Additional quotes from "Price-War Dynamics in a Free-Market Economy of Software Agents," by J. Kephart, J. Hanson, and J. Sairamesh, available at www. research.ibm.com.

CHAPTER THREE

Pages 71–73, 84: Interview with Shawn Haynes, director of the Amazon.com Associates Program, July 1998.

Pages 74–75, 84–85: Interview with James Marciano, of Refer-It.com, July 1998.

Pages 77–78: Interview with Phillip Rose, of the Lobster Net and ProActive Marketing Inc., July 1998.

Page 78: The quote from Phil Polishook, vice president of eToys, is from a story by Elizabeth Horowitt, published in *Computerworld*'s "Emmerce," July 27, 1998.

Pages 79–80: Interview with Peter Adler, president of Gallagher & Forsythe, July 1998.

Page 80: Interview with Nicole Vanderbilt of Jupiter Communications, July 1998.

Pages 85–86: Interview with TravelZoo CEO Ralph Bartel, February, 1999. For research purposes, the author became one of the 700,000 shareholders of TravelZoo. Information about them is gleaned from financial reports published at TravelZoo. com and e-mailed shareholder correspondence from the company.

Page 87: Interview with Lisa Kohring, from One and Only Personals, July 1998.

Pages 89–91: Interview with Andrew Collins, vice president at Thingworld.com (formerly Parable Corp.), August 1998.

CHAPTER FOUR

Pages 93–100, 113: Interviews with Neil Budde, editor of the *Wall Street Journal Interactive,* June 1998, plus Budde talk given at MIT Sloan School of Management class, February 1998, and follow-up e-mail exchanges, Fall 1998.

Page 98: The 19.5-minute-per-month figure for average monthly browsing at the *New York Times* site comes from "Making People Pay Online," by James Ledbetter, *The Industry Standard,* November 9, 1998.

Pages 100–105: A conversation with Erik Brynjolfsson, associate professor at MIT, February 1998. Quotes also selected from two working papers: "Bundling Information Goods: Pricing, Profits and Efficiency," December 1996, and "Aggregation and Disaggregation of Information: Implications for Bundling, Site Licensing and Micropayment Systems Goods," June 1997, both by Y. Bakos and E. Brynjolfsson. Papers have been linked from the course syllabus page at web.mit.edu/ecom/Spring1998/

Page 103: Mary Modahl quote from "Web Watcher's Formula: Spicy Opinions, Few Models," in the *Wall Street Journal,* February 19, 1998, p. B1.

Pages 107–108: Opinion of judge of the U.S. Court of Appeals for the District of Columbia, in the case of the United States vs. Microsoft, quoted in "Slice and Dice," by Louis Menand, the *New Yorker,* March 16, 1998, p. 4.

Page 110: James J. Cramer, of TheStreet.com, quoted in *Upside* interview (November 1998), 70.

Pages 110–112: Martin Nisenholtz presentation to a Harvard Business School class, February 1998.

CHAPTER FIVE

Pages 117–121: Guided tour of Dell Computer Corp.'s Metric 12 factory for desktop computers, Austin, Texas, April 1998.

Page 119: "The Power of Virtual Integration: An Interview with Michael Dell," *Harvard Business Review* (March-April 1998), p. 72.

Pages 122–123, 133: Interview with Everett Ehrlich, October 1998. Additional quotes are from Ehrlich's commentary on National Public Radio's *Morning Edition,* July 16, 1998.

Pages 122–123: "Auto Makers Beat Glut with Extras, Innovations," by Gregory L. White et al., the *Wall Street Journal,* January 8, 1998, p. 1.

Pages 125–128: Visit to Seven Cycles Inc. factory, Watertown, Massachussetts, and interviews with CEO Rob Vandermark and staff, June 1998.

Pages 128–131: Interview with Amar Goel, cofounder of Chip Shot Golf, June 1998.

Page 132: Interview with Debbie Newman of Music Boulevard, who left the company after it merged with CDnow.

Page 134: "Is This the Factory of the Future?" by Saul Hansell, the *New York Times,* Money & Business section, July 26, 1998, p. 1.

Page 135: Larry Ellison's comment made in keynote speech at the Harvard Conference on the Internet and Society, May 26, 1998.

Chapter Six

Pages 137–139: "Take-Out Data: Instill Sells E-commerce, Trend Information," by Clinton Wilder, *InformationWeek,* October 19, 1998, p. 137. Additional company information from case studies and trade press reports found at instill.com.

Pages 140–146: Bill Porter, founder of E*Trade, keynote speech at the annual MIT $50K Entrepreneurship Competition event, Cambridge, Massachussetts, May 7, 1998. Interview with Kathy Levinson, president of E*Trade Securities, October 1997. Customer acquisition figures from various press reports.

Pages 146–147: "Merrill Says Online Trading Is Bad for

Investors," by Rebecca Buckman, the *Wall Street Journal,* September 23, 1998, p. C1.

Page 149: "The Phynancier," a profile of David E. Shaw, by Thomas Bass, *Wired* (January 1997), p. 152. Note: In early 1999, Merrill said it would acquire Shaw's online brokerage.

Pages 151–152: Presentation by Tom Ashbrook, CEO of HomePortfolio, at the Harvard Conference on the Internet and Society, May 26, 1998.

Pages 152–157: Interview with Robert Stevens, president of ImproveNet, June 1998.

CHAPTER SEVEN

Pages 159–163: Interview with Matt Hyde, REI's director of online sales, October 1998.

Page 164: Interview with Jeff Bezos, founder of Amazon.com, September 1996.

Pages 165–166: Interviews with Kip Jacobson and Dana Brigham at Brookline Booksmith, October and November 1998.

Pages 171–173: Interviews with Tom Lebsack and Jonathan Adams, of Schlumberger, October 1998.

Page 174: Interview with Philip Yen, senior vice president of chip cards at Visa International, March 1998.

Pages 175–177: Quotes from Sun Microsystems executives are from Sun's press event—simulcast live on the Web—announcing its Jini connection technology, January 25, 1999.

Page 176: MIT Media Laboratory professor Neil Gershenfeld's quote is from his book *When Things Start to Think* (Henry Holt, 1999).

Page 176: Interview with Dave Leeper, Motorola's director of personal area networking, February 1999.

Page 177: Quote from Ronald Whittier, Intel senior vice

president, is from "Toys Learn a Number of Tricks in Surprising Place: Silicon Valley," by Dean Takahashi, the *Wall Street Journal*, February 8, 1999.

Pages 177–182: Visit to the U.S. Open tennis championships, September 1998. Interviews with and presentations by IBM executives Elizabeth Primrose-Smith and Jeff Ramminger as well as Mark Hardie of Forrester Research.

Epilogue

Pages 185–188: Tim Berners-Lee talk at a Cambridge, Massachussetts, breakfast hosted by *Technology Review* magazine, December, 1998. Also, an interview with Berners-Lee, October 1996.

Pages 186–187: Marc Andreessen talk at the Massachussetts Software Council meeting, April 1998.

Page 188: Interview with Alan Kay at Apple Computer headquarters, March 1994.

Pages 189–190: *River Out of Eden: A Darwinian View of Life* (Basic Books, 1995), by Richard Dawkins.

INDEX

INDEX

Shopbots, problem of, for dynamic
  pricing strategy, 65–69
Silverman, Henry, 40–41
Slate, 109
Sloan, Alfred, 188
Smart cards, 168–75
  as answer to fraud, 169–70
  in closed communities, 171
  increasing microprocessor
    power of, 170–71
  marketing ideas using,
    172–75
Smart paper, 176
Smartsuite software, 105, 106
Smith, Adam, 188
Smith, James A., 195–99
Snap, 15, 16, 67
Softbank, 145
Software, bundling and
  integration of, 105–8
Solution branding, 21–43
  branding in mass media and
    on Web, 31–35
  changes in market
    environment and viability
    of, 38–42
  characteristics of strong
    brands and, 35–38
  consumer habits and
    successful, 30–31
  quest for, in online grocery
    shopping market, 21–24
  successful creation of, in
    online grocery shopping,
    26–29
  technology fixation vs., in
    online grocery shopping,
    24–26
  websites practicing, 207–8

South Park cartoon program, 90
Sports events, integration of
  information technology at,
  177–82
Start-up companies on Web,
  9–12, 191
Steffens, John "Launny," 146,
  147
Stevens, Robert, 153, 156
Stock trading online, 10,
  140–49
  entry of giant companies into,
    146–49
  environmental changes in,
    144–46
  innovation of E*Trade in,
    140–44
Streamline company, 26–29
Subscriptions
  to online publications,
    94–100, 108–10, 113
  to Streamline online grocery
    service, 28
Sun Microsystems, 175–77
Suretrade, 142, 149
Swatch Group, The, 123–24
Swiss Army depot, 79
Syms clothing, pricing model of,
  57–58

T

Take-overs of Web companies,
  16
Technological change, effect of, on
  Web evolution, 14–15
Technology-mediated financial
  services, 149
Telecommunications capacity,
  dynamic pricing of, 44–50

225